WHEELS AND WAVES

WHEELS AND WAVES
A Cruise, Ferry, River, and Canal Barge Guide
for the Physically Handicapped

GENIE & GEORGE AROYAN

WHEELS AWEIGH PUBLISHING COMPANY
Fort Myers Beach, Florida

PUBLISHER'S CATALOGUING IN PUBLICATION DATA

Aroyan, Genie.
    Wheels and waves: cruise, ferry, river and canal barge guide for the physically handicapped / Genie & George Aroyan.

    p. cm.
    Includes index.
    LCCN: 93-93757
    ISBN: 0-9635698-0-5 (Soft cover)
            0-9635698-1-3 (Hard cover)
    1. Travel. 2. Physically handicapped--Travel.

    I. Aroyan, George F.   II Title.

HV3022.A77 1993   910.240816

Manufactured in the United States of America

10 9 8 7 6 5 4 3 2 1

WHEELS AWEIGH PUBLISHING COMPANY
17105 San Carlos Blvd., Suite A-6107, Ft. Myers Beach, FL 33931

To: *The Jonathon Livingston Seagulls of today*
Who, with some bumps along the way,
Still are up, and ready to roll,
Ashore, a-wing, or . . . afloat.

Bon voyage and happy sailing.

TABLE OF CONTENTS

CHARTS AND MAPS

ILLUSTRATIONS

TABLES

ACKNOWLEDGMENT

Most ferry and cruise line operators were especially helpful in providing ship and accessibility data on all their ships as well as some of the illustrations used herein. For an overall, broader perspective of the cruise and ferry industries, however, the annual *Guide* by Ferryconsultation was most convenient and authoritative.[1] The bimonthly *Cruise/Ferry Info* magazine was also most helpful for staying abreast of the industry's frequent name or ownership changes and the many refurbishments of the thousand large ferries and cruise ships themselves.[2]

Knight's *Modern Seamanship* was helpful for some ship descriptors in Appendix C as well as the wind force and sea tables in Appendix D.[3] An especially excellent source for a historical perspective of sea travel was B. W. Bathe's *Seven Centuries of Sea Travel*.[4]

As noted in Part V, several organizations and travel agencies, often with physically handicapped principals themselves, have long served the specialized needs of handicapped travelers. The Hoffmans of Evergreen Travel, for example, have arranged such trips and cruises for some 30-odd years; the Jacobson's of Flying Wheels Travel for a quarter of a century, and Janice Perkins of Hinsdale Travel for more than a dozen years. Most noteworthy too, are the Nau's of Nautilus Tours (and President of Travel Industry & Disabled Exchange), who as architects and now leading tour organizers, have worked effectively to eliminate handicapped barriers.

For 27 tears, the Society for Advancement of Travel for the Handicapped (SATH) has provided useful information for handicapped travelers often reporting on shipboard travel problems. The Handicapped Travel Newsletter has also often commented on cruise travel through their Editor Dr. Michael Quigley's frequent cruises (including his good advocacy overview article in *Guide '91*).[1]

Renowned for a broader undertaking, Helen Hecker (RN, Author and Publisher of Twin Peaks Press) has long worked with handicapped travelers, networking nurses to aid or accompany them, and further writing and distributing books of interest to handicapped persons.

Especially noteworthy, too, are Mr. Tom Gilbert's pioneering efforts of personally inspecting and making available to all, his reports on the detailed accessibility of many ocean cruise vessels calling on U. S. ports.

Most technically current today is Mr. Kevin Anthoney, who with tape measure and wide-angle lensed camera in hand, has carefully documented the critical measurements of some 70-odd cruise ships. The , has aAn excellent detailed summary of some of these measurements are listed in theJan/Feb 1993 issue of *Cruise Travel* magazine.[5]

As most knowledgeable active consultants, the addresses of both Mr. Anthoney and Mr. Gilbert are noted in Part V along with the addresses of other travel agencies and organizations specializing on the handicapped.

Supplementing our own inspection efforts from many voyages on all sizes and types of ships, were the replies to the detailed questionnaires sent to the various ferry and cruise ship operators which are gratefully acknowledged. Always helpful, but perhaps misled by the many in wheelchairs who can stand and walk a few steps, the cruise lines had often designated their most suitable cabins as "handicapped" though often they were inaccessible to a completely wheelchair-dependent person. Most new ships, however, do have accessible cabins that follow a new international ship-building standard.

Lastly, the authors wish to acknowledge the consummate skills of Mr. Ray C. McCormack who, through one author's life, had transformed his most difficult technical engineering treatises into grammatically correct language understandable to many. Though little of that may have rubbed off, the added humor of his many playful deprecating notes is gratefully acknowledged by dedicating the Glossary to him.

Guiding us through many early publishing problems, the kind and most helpful advice of Mr. John Daniel of Fithian Press is also gratefully acknowledged.

[1] *Guide '90, '91, '92, & '93,* Plus 2, Ferryconsultation, P.O. Box 7067, S-300 07 Halmstad, Sweden

[2] *Cruise Ferry Info,* (Bi-monthly '91 to '93), Marine Trading AB Brogatan 7, S-302 42 Halmstad, Sweden

[3] Knight's Modern Seamanship, Van Nostrand Rheinhold, 450 West 33rd Street, New York, NY 10001

[4] *Seven Centuries of Sea Travel*, B.W. Bathe, Crown Books, NY

[5] *Cruise Travel* Magazine, World Publishing Company, 990 Grove St. 4th Floor, Evanston, IL 60210-4370

PUBLISHER'S NOTE

Every effort was made to ensure the accuracy and timeliness of the data presented herein. However, the travel, ferry, and especially the cruise industry change frequently, measurements are not always made accurately, and inadvertent transcribing, typesetting and other errors can be introduced during the publishing process. This book should therefore be used as a guide rather than as a definitive handbook, and neither authors nor publisher can be held responsible for the occasional errors that may appear.

Many factors useful to handicapped persons are nonetheless included. But since each person's handicap and preferences differ so widely, only the most serious obstacles blocking passage to wheelchairs are emphazised.

Ship operators do require advance notification of any physical handicap, or other health or special diet requirements of the traveler. They further reserve the right to deny passage to anyone whose voyage they judge may present a health, comfort, or safety problem for either the traveler himself or his fellow passengers, or may place an undue burden on the lines themselves.

Any statements, opinions, or judgements by the authors are theirs alone and made without prejudice. Comments, corrections and other helpful suggestions would be most welcome by both authors and publisher.

WHEELS AWEIGH PUBLISHING COMPANY
17105 San Carlos Blvd., #A-6107
Fort Myers Beach, FL 33931

INTRODUCTION

Ships challenge the handicapped. No elevators on the smallest of ships, and, excepting suites, tiny cabins and inaccessible bathrooms for most others.

The accessibility of many types of ships are discussed here. Most large new ferries and cruise ships have good handicapped facilities. But on many other smaller and older ones, the bathrooms are not accessible to those who cannot walk a few steps. Some spokespersons say "some assistance" or "limited mobility" is required, both meaning it is not accessible to wheelchairs.

The newer handicapped staterooms may have 30" to 40" wide door openings with very negligible sills. But other "handicapped-designated" cabins have only 22" to 24" wide openings to the bathrooms with very high entry sills. Those entries will not pass regular wheelchairs, but they are far better than the impossibly small standard shipboard cabins with less than 20" wide openings and towering 6" to 9" high sills.

The coamings (sills) around hatches and door openings to all outside decks are particularly difficult to manage. Invented by designers of the Great Wall of China, the coamings are meant to keep water out on deck or from running freely around below. They block you at every turn; trip people who walk too! Pass those hurdles however, and with everything at hand, it was, and is, paradise, paradise afloat. A great way to travel!

And people do. The world's four and a half million annual passenger cruise ship market dominated by Americans has half the world's cruise fleet operating from U.S. ports. But elsewhere in the world, some hundreds of millions of travelers flock to the ferries every year to visit neighboring islands, countries, or to coast along their rocky or mountainous shores. Bringing one's handicapped-equipped car or van along is a big bonus for the handicapped.

More tranquil but far fewer, and by and large less accessible, are the many overnight river boats and hotel-like canal barges found in some parts of the world.

But over-water travel isn't for everyone, handicapped or not. Some give and take is needed; hospital ships they are not. Many cabins marked as handicapped aren't that well suited for those who cannot walk at all. However, some are, and **most new** ships **do** have accessible cabins . . . with low sills there and elsewhere in all public rooms. With refurbishment, older ships too, are becoming more accessible.

To assist handicapped travelers in assessing their own difficulty, the critical limiting stateroom and bathroom door widths and sill heights are included in many of the ship listings that follow. Elsewhere aboard ship, helpful crew members are always nearby for an assist when needed.

Finally, for ships, safety at sea considerations reign supreme. Fair-weather cruising areas, anti-roll stabilizers, direct satellite weather reports and good weather radar to bypass stormy regions all help. But the wind and sea are their own masters; bad weather or angry seas will dampen the most ebullient of spirits and roil the best of plans.

Some History

The seas seduce us. Lakes and rivers, too. Half of all Americans live within 50 miles of a coast. Add in the other seas, lakes, and rivers of the world, and the whole world and all its civilizations are then but a stone's splash or surf's sound away from water, and . . . some type of boat.

As today, the most ancient of civilizations had their boats; 4000 B.C. on the Nile for the Egyptians, and on to the Euphrates, Indus, and the vast rivers of China for the other early civilizations. Where there were no connecting waters, they dug canals. China's 1000 mile long Grand Canal was built between 605 and 610 A.D. to connect Beijing with Shanghai. And France bypassed the Straits of Gibralter with the Midi Canal 300 years ago to connect its western Atlantic shores to the Mediterranean.

But it was the steamships of the Industrial Age that brought regular schedules and put the world within easy reach of all. Robert Fulton's first steamboat ride on the Hudson in 1807 was followed a dozen years later by *Savannah's* first Atlantic crossing in 1819.

It was another 21 years before Nova Scotia's Samuel Cunard, in 1840, established scheduled transatlantic steamer voyages on the *Brittania* for regular mail (pacquet) and passenger service. They were long crossings; with the Westerlies and the Gulf Stream, an average 24 days east, and 38 days west. But these regular sailings brought on the great ocean liners with ever larger and faster (five day crossings) ships until a few years past the end of World War II, when cheaper and faster jets all but killed them off.

But not for romantics who turned the bow of those large floating hotel palaces to other climes for play. Like the ancient Romans with their lakeside pleasure barges, the very wealthy had, a century ago, also cruised the Mediterrane. But some intrepid souls had even encircled the world before then. It was in the 18th century; and on a very slow boat . . . 3 years on the American built *Columbia*. But more "fame than gain," such voyages were dropped until Cunard began them again with the steam-powered, 19,680-ton *Laconia's* regularly scheduled round-the-world cruise in 1922.

But now, cruises are available for all; pleasure seekers in the sun, adventurers to the isolated corners of the world, and the growing wheel-happy auto-dependent public seeking to bring its cars along, and across any body of water. An explosion of grand ship designs, small to large, now serves every desire, style, and pocketbook.

The World's Cruising Areas

More than half of all cruises are close to home in the mild-weather Caribbean. Other popular Western Hemisphere destinations include Bermuda, both coasts of Mexico, Transcanal, and Alaska.

There are many cruises in Europe. You can cruise northward to the North Cape above the Arctic Circle or into the Baltic Sea and visit St. Petersburg, the Hermitage and European palace of the Czars. Many point south to the blue-waters of the Mediterranean and the tumultuous and fabled Near East. Others ease into Europe's heartland, and voyage down its many scenic and historic rivers and canals.

Cruises venture to other continents as well. One may voyage around Africa or circumnavigate South America, and, in '94, even Antarctica. There are cruises throughout the Far East: the Coral and Tasmanian Seas to Australia, New Zealand and the nearby South Pacific islands, or on to India in the Indian Ocean, the Seychelles, or east coast of Africa. Or for a change of pace, some join the one-in-a-million to visit Antarctica. Still others hook them all together into a world cruise, several of them.

These cruise areas are depicted in solid-lined boxes on the facing Chart I as are the regions with the highest ferry traffic shown in dotted outline. These large ferries too cross many of the world's seas and regularly visit many of these same shores. As shown, they are widely used along the entire Pacific Northwest Coast, and to Canada's Maritime Provinces. But the grandest ships and most heavily trafficked ferry routes are across the busy seas of Europe, Japan, and to a lesser extent, Southeast Asia.

Rivers at home and abroad also offer lively and interesting journeys along the great Mississippi, St. Lawrence, Snake, Columbia, and other inland waterways. Many riverboats and canal barges ease along Europe's crisscrossing rivers and canals. And the antipodes of South Australia finds the most accessible riverboat facility of all to cruise on Australia's mightiest river. Early Aussie costumed staff with some of their grub and "Waltzing Mathilda" is as much fun for an early glimpse of that country in a wheelchair, as the *Mississippi Queen* is here for the able-legged.

In the pages ahead, most of the ships with handicapped facilities are all presented along with their routes and destinations. Some heads-up tips about cruising are also presented for those who may be rolling with the waves on wheels for the first time.

Chart I
The Cruising World.

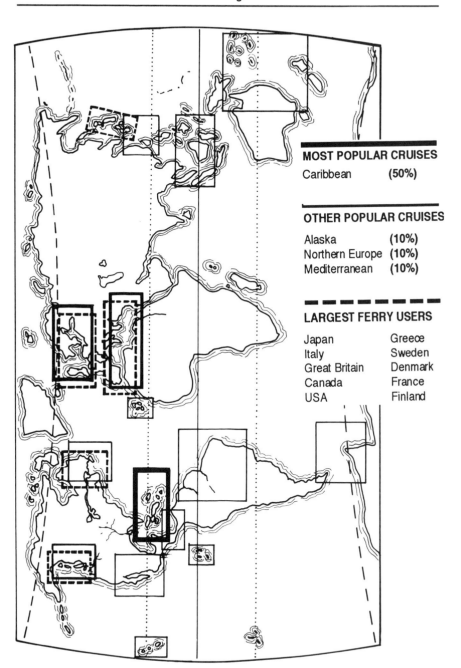

MOST POPULAR CRUISES

Caribbean   **(50%)**

OTHER POPULAR CRUISES

Alaska   **(10%)**
Northern Europe   **(10%)**
Mediterranean   **(10%)**

LARGEST FERRY USERS

Japan   Greece
Italy   Sweden
Great Britain   Denmark
Canada   France
USA   Finland

SUMMARY

Figure 1 depicts a few of the vessels described subsequently as illustrative of the wide range of size, type, and style ships in service.

The ocean liners of yesteryear majestically linked distant ports on a regular basis. So too today, do the large "super" ferries of the North and Baltic Seas link their major cities. Some of the many amenities and attractions of the most glamorous of cruise ships are now found on many of these new cruise-like ferries. There is no comparable Ritz Carlton-type dining with maitre d's and seven-course gourmet dinners, but there are duty free shops, casinos, and lively entertainment along with a variety of food malls, cafeterias, buffets, and restaurants.

These large car ferries, including those of North America and elsewhere in Europe, are described in Part I. Many have elevators and handicapped rest rooms aboard while still others have handicapped cabins for their longer overnight trips. These cabins are generally larger than standard ones however, and held until one week prior to sailing before being released to the general public.

For cruise ships, there is a very wide selection from among their many types and sizes. They range from ultra-luxury types and the most densely packed, lively, and largest ones afloat to small yacht-like and the most rugged, ice-hardened, expeditionary-type vessels in the world. Only about one fifth of them have handicapped accommodations (many of which are not accessible to standard wheelchairs), but most large new vessels do have excellent facilities.

Part II describes the best of five different types and sizes of these ships grouped together by size. The Directory at the end of that part, includes descriptions of many other ships both with, and without handicapped designated cabins per se, but with some of their individual accessibility limitations noted in the accompanying tables.

Among the hotel-like ships, but far smaller and fewer in number, are the more than 50 overnight river cruise ships and many hundreds of hotel

Figure 1
Representative Ship Types and Sizes.

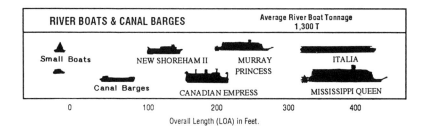

RIVER BOATS & CANAL BARGES
Average River Boat Tonnage 1,300 T

Small Boats
NEW SHOREHAM II
MURRAY PRINCESS
ITALIA
Canal Barges
CANADIAN EMPRESS
MISSISSIPPI QUEEN

0   100   200   300   400

Overall Length (LOA) in Feet.

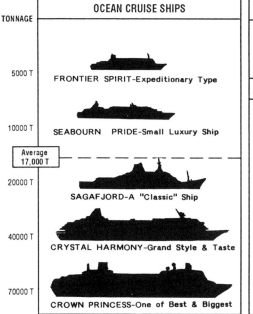

OCEAN CRUISE SHIPS

TONNAGE

5000 T   FRONTIER SPIRIT-Expeditionary Type

10000 T   SEABOURN PRIDE-Small Luxury Ship

Average 17,000 T

20000 T   SAGAFJORD-A "Classic" Ship

40000 T   CRYSTAL HARMONY-Grand Style & Taste

70000 T   CROWN PRINCESS-One of Best & Biggest

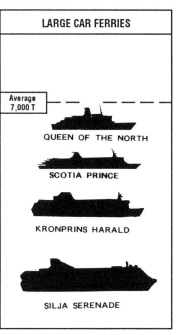

LARGE CAR FERRIES

Average 7,000 T

QUEEN OF THE NORTH

SCOTIA PRINCE

KRONPRINS HARALD

SILJA SERENADE

canal barges, few of which are completely accessible to those who cannot stand or walk. A few that are completely accessible, and others with elevators and better-than- average accessibility, are described in more detail in Part III.

Australia's *Murray Princess* has a proper elevator as do a few American ones. Elsewhere in the world, however, the Old World's bridges limit the heights of river and canal boats. With few decks, elevators are rare. The few river cruise boats and canal barges with elevators or railing attached seat lifts between decks, or which have upper deck cabins on the main lounge and dining decks, are also included in the accompanying tables.

The ships with good handicapped facilities represent the cream of the crop. The ships are often newer, and the ship operators who provide those good facilities and give it some attention, are the best in the industry. Others, paying little attention to the well-being of the handicapped, often fall short in their treatment of other passenger too. They are not first class.

All of these ships, together with their various cruise areas, are listed in the pages ahead. Part I covers the ferries, Part II cruise ships, and Part III, river boats and canal barges. Part IV adds a few pages on self help and for charter boats. In addition to the small sail and power boats, two fully accessible large sailing vessels are described where handicapped passengers join the regular small crew to sail the vessel.

Vessels engaged in short day excursions and freighters carrying a dozen passengers or less, are not included. The latter are not accessible. The voyages may be long, and they are neither well serviced by elevators nor have a doctor on board.

Finally, Part V adds more light on the handicapped accommodations found aboard ship along with helpful tips from our own half-century of sailing to six of the world's continents in all sized ships. Old-fashioned guts, adaptability, and above all, a sense of humor were the words of the day a dozen years ago when there were no totally wheelchair-accessible cabins. These tips touch on cabin selection, preparations before boarding, once on board, and also how to get around those "inaccessible" shore excursions and other unanticipated barriers.

Also included are four appendices. Appendix A describes devices to temporarily narrow your chair as well as a number of narrow wheelchairs that may be rented for those ships that need them. Appendix B briefly describes some of the Department of Transportation's proposed rules in furtherance of the Americans with Disabilities Act which have focused primarily on ferries and their terminals for shipboard travel since so few of the world's ships are American flagged. Appendix C contains some overall general background information on different types of boats and ships with some of their shipboard equipment. Finally, in Appendix D, sea states, and the winds that cause them, are briefly characterized. With tongue in cheek, a Glossary lists common nautical terms. An Index follows.

A wide range of sizes

There is wide selection of ship sizes, classes, and styles from which to choose. They range from those serving a dozen passengers or less on some canal barges, to large skyscraper or resort-like cruise ships and ferries that can accommodate a few thousand overnight guests.

Excepting the large new cruise ships and "super" ferries, most passenger vessels today are smaller than the Transatlantic liners of yesteryear built to weather the North Atlantic's fierce winter storms. Even in 1912, the *Titanic* was an impressive 60,000 tons. In 1935, the *Normandie,* the world's largest till then at 79,300 tons, was followed shortly by the largest cruise ship ever, the 81,235 ton *Queen Mary.* Only now is an American behemoth of a cruise ship being built (the *Phoenix*) that will, in a few years, dwarf those others by a large margin.

But the sizes of ships need some explanation. Numbers of passengers are understood readily enough, but tonnage needs a word.

The Navies of the world use weight or displacement to measure a ship's size, but the maritime industry uses a measure of a ship's enclosed **volume** as a measure of its potential payload carrying capacity (port fees are charged accordingly). Known as "gross registered tons" or g.r.t., these capacity measures were once nominally made equivalent to 100 ft^3. By international agreement, that factor now varies from 110 to 160 ft^3 per ton depending on height of freeboard, size, type of ship, etc.

A ship's spaciousness therefore may be determined by dividing the tonnage by the number of passengers to obtain a measure of cubic feet per passenger (which includes crew space, passageways, public rooms, etc.).

The spaciousness, or tonnage per passenger, varies more than a factor of two between luxury 5 star, or 5 star plus rated ships and the more crowded, popularly priced cruise ships. River boats and higher density, shorter crossing time ferries, also have less room per passenger.

The wide range of numbers of passengers carried by these various types and sizes of vessels in each category is illustrated in Figure 2. Not surprisingly, the largest ships are ocean-going cruise ships which average 17,000 tons. Smaller on average, but also crossing many seas in all types of weather, ferries average 6,700 tons. Operating in the most sheltered and restricted of waters, river boats are smallest averaging but 1300 tons. Passenger density may be estimated as noted in the illustration or can be found in the more descriptive tables and text that follow.

Figure 2
Range of Numbers of Passengers Carried in Each Size and Type Ship
with Sample Ships Discussed.

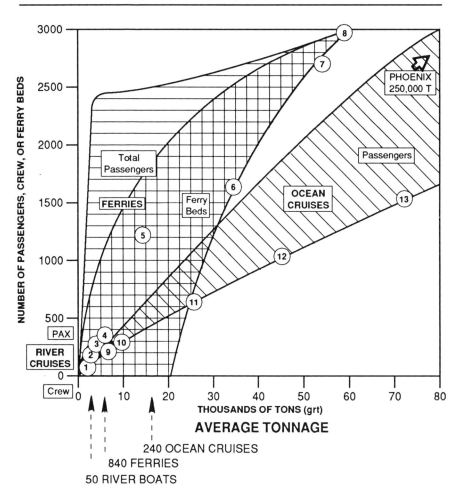

RIVER/ CANAL BARGES	FERRIES	OCEAN CRUISE SHIPS
1. DIONYSOS	5. SCOTIA PRINCE	9. FRONTIER SPIRIT
2. ITALIA &	6. KRONPRINS HARALD	10. SEABOURN SPIRIT
MURRAY PRINCESS	7. SILJA SERENADE	11. SAGAFJORD
3. MISSISSIPPI QUEEN	8. SILJA EUROPA	12. CRYSTAL HARMONY
4. AMERICAN QUEEN		13. CROWN PRINCESS

PART I
FERRIES

Want to visit Ireland, the Greek islands, St. Petersburg; or see Norway's fjords or an Alaskan glacier at less than half the cost of a cruise? Then catch a ferry, an accessible one, and take your car . . . the hand-control equipped one . . . along too! In Europe, of course, rent one .

In total, there are more than three times as many over 1000-ton car ferries as all the cruise ships combined. But the ferries are more crowded, less formal, and less elegant than cruise ships. They do, however, have many of the same amenities aboard: bars, lounges, live entertainment, a number of dining choices, and, if between nations, duty-free shops and a casino.

On the smallest of open ferries, with crossings of 15 minutes or so, there are no public facilities of any sort and you must remain on the car deck. Advise the staff of your handicap when lining up for the wait. You will be boarded either first or last where there is room to open the door, and get out on deck to watch the crossing from a better vantage point.

On larger ferries, however, passengers are not allowed on the car decks. Accessible elevators are found convenient to handicapped parking on many of these long distance ferries. On one upper deck are buffets, grills and several dining areas, and, on the largest long distance ferries, the large panoply of attractions and services found on large cruise ships. There too, you will find handicapped public bathrooms, and elsewhere, on the largest new ships, wheelchair-accessible cabins.

Best of all, you can drive on and off the ferry to continue your journey with ease and without the discomfort of fighting local crowds and wrestling with public transportation.

The average car ferry of 6,700 tons carries a few hundred cars and a thousand day passengers. For overnight journeys, they can often only berth half that number in tiny cabins. But the largest and most magnificent ferries which have entered service in the North and Baltic Seas have good facilities for all passengers.

The 58,000 ton *Silja Serenade* and *Silja Symphony* serve the route between Sweden and Finland. Each ship sleeps 2614 passengers and carries 450 cars with another half mile of lane space for trucks. Equally important, there are 12 good handicapped cabins aboard each vessel.

Joining them in '93 is the largest ferry of all; the new 59,000 ton, 3000 passenger *Silja Europa*. The glass-domed, six-story atrium, glass elevators, and sparkling decor place it with the most spectacular of new cruise ships. The best live entertainment warms the Baltic air in this "Theater Ship's" Moulin Rouge. Some part with money in the casino, others in the large duty-free shopping arcades. The first McDonald's to go to sea is adjacent to a video arcade room for the young. Elsewhere, there are many dining alternatives: a Food Mart, Italian, grilled and Swedish delights.

Although Japan has more ferries and higher traffic than any other nation, most of the world's fleet is in Europe. Finland's 13 large ferries average an impressive 27,000 tons, Sweden's 30-odd, 18,000 tons, while France's two dozen average a still large, 14,000 tons.

Half the world's fleet operates in the Mediterranean, but those ferries are generally smaller. Smaller still are the U.S.'s 26 over one thousand ton car ferries which average only 2,400 tons.

In the next two sections, illustrations and charts of the larger North American and European car ferries and their routes are all briefly summarized. The ferry operators and those ferries with elevators and accessible public restrooms (or with handicapped overnight accommodations), are also briefly summarized and grouped together at the end of this section for more convenient subsequent reference.

As in the U.S., handicap-controlled cars and vans can be rented in Europe. Avis has them in Frankfurt, Germany and in Switzerland; Hertz in Great Britain and Spain. Auto Europe too, has such cars in Germany. In England, Mobility Car Rental, Meon Car Hire, and Wheelchair Travel Ltd. have cars or vans for rent, but frequently limit their use to Britain only.

NORTH AMERICAN FERRIES

Canada's 44 large car ferries represent the world's seventh largest fleet of ferries; they serve British Columbia in the west, Quebec and the Maritime Provinces to the East. Ninth in the world, the U.S. fleet serves principally the San Juan Islands and sheltered waterways of Puget Sound, and Alaska's long inside passage. Mexico's small fleet of 5 ferries bridging the Gulf of California represents the world's 35th largest capacity, but like those of many other less advanced nations, they are not accessible.

Elsewhere in the U.S., car ferries have long operated across Lake Michigan and Lake Champlain, with a new Lake Erie route currently in the planning stage. On the East Coast, they are found from FDR's Campobello Island at the tip of Maine to Nantucket and the Kennedy's Martha's Vineyard. Further south, ferries cross the Hudson in New York and other large open bays or estuaries, such as the Delaware. There are small ferries across the entrance to Mobile Bay and to North Carolina's off-shore banks.

The many passenger-only commuter ferries to excursion areas like the Statue of Liberty or Ellis Island in NY, Cuttyhunk Island in Massachusetts, some of Maine's many islands, Mackinac Island in Lake Huron, Isle Royale National Park in Lake Superior, Catalina near Los Angeles, etc. are not discussed here. There are also many short, passenger-only commuter ferries to beat the traffic and parking problems of large waterbound communities like Sidney, Hong Kong, Istanbul, Halifax, etc. Despite its magnificent soaring bridges, San Francisco still has those lowly, down-to-earth ferries operating from Tiburon, from Larkspur Landing in San Rafael, and from Oakland since the '89 earthquake.

Large car ferries blossom forth in summer vacationlands. One-hour, 45-minute accessible car ferries cross Lake Huron from Tobermory to South Baymouth, Ontario, on Manitoulin Island (the largest fresh-water island in the world), to Beaver Island from Charlevoix, MI, some of Maine's islands and additional routes in Canada's Maritime Provinces.

Short ferry crossings are no problem for the handicapped, but handicapped facilities are required on journeys exceeding a few hours. Alaska's Marine Highway journey can run up to three days, while the Labrador run also exceeds one day.

Except for the shortest of ferry crossings, most ferry buildings or terminals at either end of the journey in Canada or the U.S., are accessible. Others soon will be, to comply with the Americans with Disabilities Act as noted in Appendix B.

West Coast Ferries

Washington State's 19 ferries are day sailors (half priced for the handicapped). But as noted in Table 1 (p.30), only the larger, newer ones have elevators (as does Black Ball Transport's *Coho* serving the seven-hour crossing from Port Angeles direct to Victoria, B.C.).

The routes of these ferries, and the others to British Columbia and Alaska are shown in Chart II. Of BC Ferries' 38 ships, 16 have cafeterias and washrooms for the disabled, but only 14 of them have elevators, with the other two requiring boarding on a different deck. The West Coast routes of BC ferries and those of the State of Alaska are all listed in Table 2 (p.31), along with the ferries with elevators and accessible washrooms.

On longer journeys along the British Columbia and Alaskan coasts, BC Ferries has two overnight ferries with beds, but only one of those is accessible (*Queen of the North*). All of the five ships operated by the State of Alaska's Marine Highway System, however, have elevators with good wheelchair access to dining rooms, handicapped toilet facilities, and special handicapped overnight cabins. No traveling companion is required on any of these latter vessels but is recommended for the smaller *Tustumena*, where certain routes can encounter rough seas. All of Alaska Marine Highways are very popular; reservations must be made well in advance.

Chart II
U.S. & Canadian Pacific Coast Ferries

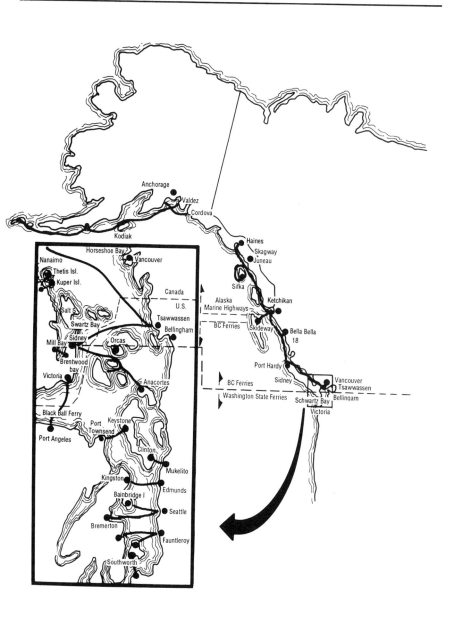

Great Lakes to Eastern Seaboard Ferries

Many ferries once crossed Lake Michigan 100 years ago avoiding the Chicago snarl when roads were poor and rail links few. Railroad magnate Cornelius Vanderbilt even earned his "commodore" sobriquet because of the large fleet of ferries he operated. Although plans are being made to introduce a new ferry line from Milwaukee, today, only the 4,244 ton, refurbished, older, coal burning reciprocating steamship *Badger* (former train ferry and once the world's largest) now crosses the narrow waist of Lake Michigan on its four hour journey between Manitowoc, WI, and Ludington, MI. Movies, a museum, arcade, snacks, buffets and beverages are all available. Available for loan, too, is one narrow wheelchair.

The *Badger's* restrooms are fully accessible to standard wheelchairs as are its 42 cabins for narrower 22" ones for those wishing more privacy. Although the cabins are not advertised as accessible, they have no sills into the cabins nor into the private toilet facility.

In Canada, the *Chi-Cheemaun* and *Nindawayma* cross Lake Huron from Tobermory, Ontario, to South Baymouth on Manitoulin Island, with elevators and accessible bathrooms aboard. An occasional ferry crosses the Tennessee and Mississippi Rivers, even with bridges not too distant. Farther east, three car ferries trisect Lake Champlain.

The year-round ferries from Quebec to Delaware Bay depicted in Chart III, and noted in Tables 3 and 4 (pp 32 & 33), are, for the most part, accessible.

From the States, the Prince of Fundy's *Scotia Prince* serves the 11-hour overnight trip from Portland, ME to Yarmouth, Nova Scotia, with duty-free shopping, live entertainment, lounges, bars, video game room for the young, regular casino, and many slot machines for the gamblers.

The movies and outside decks are not accessible to wheelchairs. But there are two relatively large (for ferries) inside handicapped accessible cabins aboard the *Scotia Prince* as noted in Figure 3. Nominally 4-person cabins (with fold-down bunks), they are used as doubles for the handicapped. There are no sills through the 33" entry doors, and a portable ramp is used over the 7" sill into the roll-in shower. As on most ferries, powered wheelchairs are allowed, but there are 3" to 4" fire door sills.

Chart III
Large East Coast Car Ferries

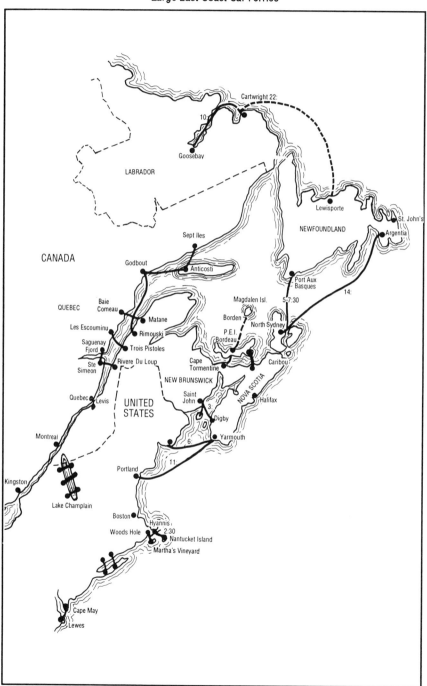

The route from Yarmouth, Nova Scotia to Bar Harbor, Maine on Marine Atlantic's accessible *Bluenose* is a shorter trip across the Bay of Fundy. Shorter still is the trip from Digby, Nova Scotia, to Saint John, New Brunswick, on the accessible *Princess of Arcadia*..

Prince Edward Island (P.E.I.) is served year round from Cape Tormentine, New Brunswick, but only from April to December between Caribou, Nova Scotia and the P.E.I.'s eastern town of Borden. In any case, you pay only to get off the island on the ships whose accessibility was noted earlier in Table 4.

There are accessible facilities on the *Lucy Maud Montgomery* ("Anne of Green Gables") ferry to Quebec's Magdalen Islands from Souris, Prince Edward Island.

Five of Marine Atlantic's seven ferries with overnight cabins are accessible. The other ten large ones with no overnight facilities have cafeterias, elevators, and accessible public bathrooms.

Crossing times vary from less than a couple of hours on some short runs to 14 hours between Nova Scotia and Newfoundland. It's even longer to Labrador, taking upwards of 30 hours from Newfoundland. The sisterships *Caribou* and *Joseph & Carla Smallwood* serve the longer Newfoundland Island route from North Sydney, Nova Scotia with accessible overnight cabins. They also have accessible bar lounges, as do most others.

Figure 3
Deck Plans of the SCOTIA PRINCE

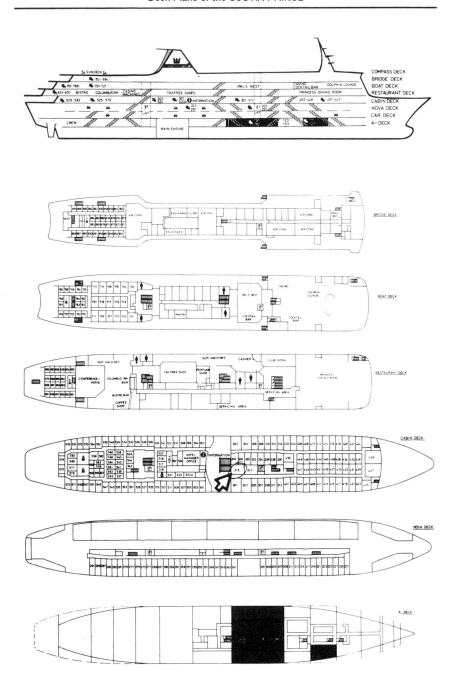

EUROPEAN FERRIES

Ferries provide a critical transportation link throughout Europe. They carry the commerce between the Continent and the British Isles, and bond all of the Scandinavian countries together as well as to their other Continental neighbors. Further south, ferries are the lifeblood of the Mediterranean.

In all, approximately 500 large ferries operate in Europe under more than 100 different ferry line operators. The couple of dozen operators that dominate certain markets with a dozen ferries or more, are described here, beginning with those serving the British Isles and the Continent. The Scandinavian ferries are then discussed, followed by those in the Mediterranean.

Small operators with three ferries or less, are not included but they generally operate on short runs of a few hours or less which may not be all that troublesome for the handicapped.

British Isles and Channel Crossings

The routes between the British Isles and the Continent are shown in Chart IV with abbreviations of the major seaports listed later in Table 5 (p.34). Accessible public bathrooms are commonly found in most of these terminals and many of the larger ships that serve these routes.

In England, for example, the large new ferries serving Shetland and the Western Isles of Scotland are accessible, with handicapped toilets on board, but many of the smaller ferries are not as well equipped. On the other hand, most of the ferries serving Ireland and the higher trafficked smaller islands (i.e., Isle of Man, Isle of Wight, and the Channel Isles) are well equipped with handicapped facilities.

Smaller, high speed ferries usually do not have wheelchair provisions, but many of the large vessels crossing the English Channel to France and Holland can accommodate wheelchairs. Still larger ships on the longer North Sea crossings to Norway and Denmark, most often also have handicapped cabins aboard.

Chart IV
Some major European Atlantic and Scandinavian ferries.

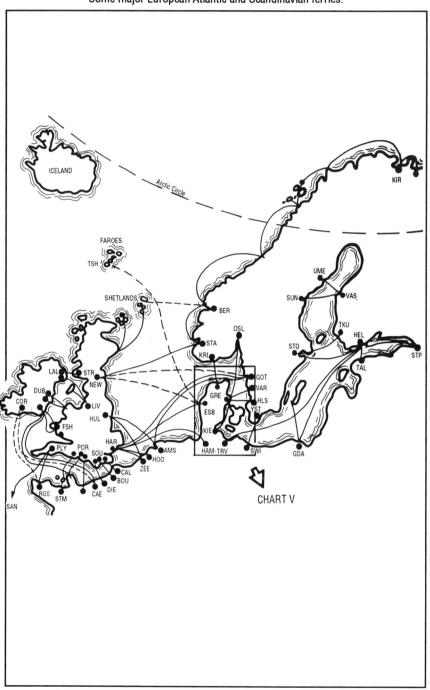

The lines and operators of the British Isle ferries themselves are all listed in Table 6 (p. 35). As with cruise ships, accessibility varies greatly among the many ferry line operators. All of P&O Ferries from Dover, Portsmouth, and Felixstowe, for example, have elevators with handicapped toilet facilities, but the Olau Line does not. Brittany Ferries has specially adapted cabins on its longer routes. Sally Line's *Sally Star* has several cabins, but doorways are only 22" wide with 2" to 3" sills.

Faster ferries (upwards of 35 knots) are frequently used on many of the shorter Channel runs. These vessels all employ unconventional hull forms and propulsion systems that do not allow much room for a wheelchair. Described more fully in Appendix C, the hovercraft that carry 30% of the Channel's passenger traffic, float on a cushion of air driven by topside propellers. Jet or hydrofoil boats have underwater wings or foils to lift the hull out of the water. But these high-speed craft, like airplanes, crowd passengers together in airline-type seats with no room for a wheelchair. The rides, moreover, may be noisy and bumpy; OK if in a hurry, but less pleasurable for true sea lovers and a real ordeal for the handicapped.

Scandinavian Ferries and Norway's Coastal Steamers

Scandinavian ferries, . . . the fairest of them all. More peaceful now than in days of yore, the Vikings still sail forth in the grandest ferries afloat to capture the Channel Coast and northern European markets as shown earlier in Chart IV, and for Denmark, in Chart V. For many of the small, winter bound communities, ferries and coastal steamers provide easier and often the only transport links to the outside world.

The Scandinavian ferries serve all of the Scandinavian countries as well as reaching out to Iceland, the Faroe Islands, England and Holland to their west. Germany, Poland, and St. Petersburg are linked to them to the south and east. Most routes are year round. Some operate only during the better, summer vacation months.

Figure 4 illustrates deck plans of two of these larger car ferries. Color Line's 31,914 ton *Kronprins Harald* and the 38,500 ton *Prinsesse Ragnhi* have six handicapped cabins each and carry 1454 and 1875 passengers

Chart V
Denmark's major ferry links in Kattegat & Skaggerak

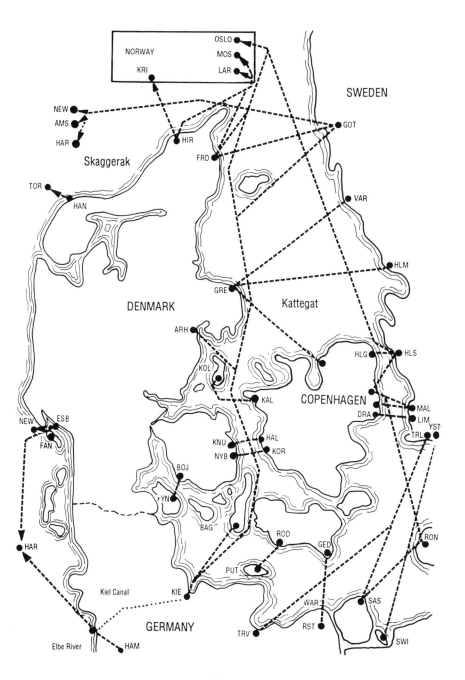

Figure 4
KRONPRINS HARALD & PRINSESSE RAGHNI

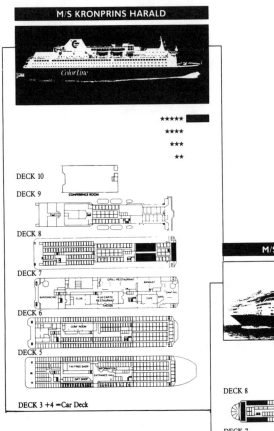

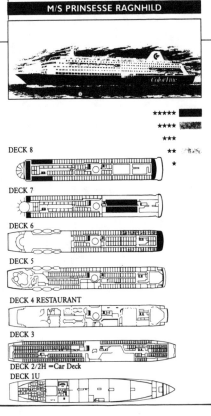

respectively, with as many beds for their overnight trips between Oslo, Norway, and Kiel, Germany. Averaging two and a half persons per car, all of their cars can be brought along (583 and 783 cars, respectively, for each of the two ships). There is also a half mile of lane space for trucks.

Table 7 (p. 36) cross references the major ferries linking these countries, and the ferry line operators or their U.S. agents. Tables 8, 9, and 10, (pp 37, 38, & 39), list the North Sea, Denmark, and the Baltic Sea ferries that have elevators and accessible public toilets aboard, as well as other longer-journey ones with handicapped sleeping accommodations.

Ships on shorter routes between neighboring countries also have lifts and handicapped public toilets.

One other popular long journey is up to the North Cape beyond the Arctic Circle (many such cruises are noted in Part II). Alternatively, however, one may board one of Norway's four newest, 4000 ton coastal steamers listed in Table 8, all with handicapped cabins and a lift between decks.

Some cars are carried (40), but no cars are needed for this 12 day, return trip. Everything of interest is within walking (rolling or bumping over cobblestones) distance. If suitable accommodations can be found, one can always stop off a few days en route.

MEDITERRANEAN CROSSINGS

The many ferry routes across the Mediterranean countries are depicted in Chart VI; the operators and their U.S. agents are listed in Table 11(p.40). Finding good handicapped facilities, however, is a problem.

Excepting France, Mediterranean countries trail the U.S., Canada, Scandinavian and Channel-crossing countries in providing good facilities for the handicapped. Squatting to use "Eastern"-style toilets found throughout the Eastern Mediterranean is still common; Western-style hotels must be sought for relief. Fortunately, they are found everywhere.

Most large Mediterranean ferries have elevators but are not otherwise well designed for the handicapped. Spain's 13 Trasmediterranea's ferries with elevators, for example, have no handicapped toilet facilities nor

Chart VI
Ferries across the Mediterranean

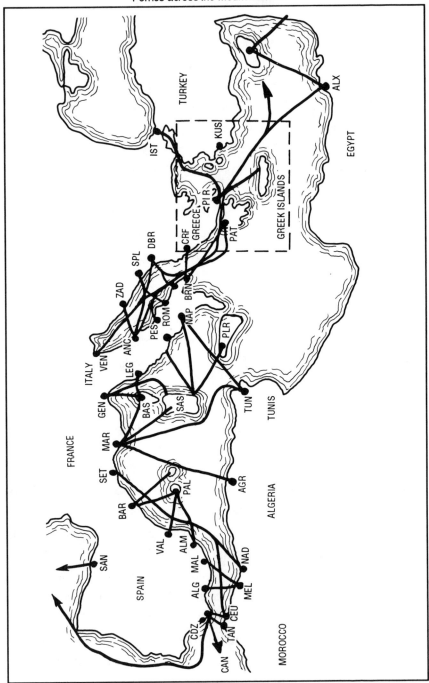

any handicapped cabins on their longer journeys to the Canary Islands.

Many Mediterranean islands, however, are but short journeys from the mainland or other nearby islands. Intrepid handicapped travelers can island hop with the locals on these ferries. Chart VII, for example, depicts some of the many routes blanketing the popular Greek Islands.

For others desiring more assurance of finding adequate facilities, Part II describes an abundance of cruise ships plying the Mediterranean. Most of the included ones listed are accessible, but most cruise ships are not (e.g. none of Greek line Epirotiki's eight ships have handicapped facilities aboard).

Chart VII

Some representative popular car ferry links to Greek Islands.

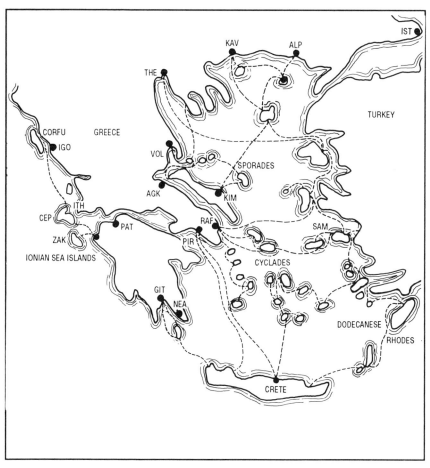

Table 1

State of Washington's car ferries with handicapped facilities.
NOTE: There are no overnight berths on Black Ball or Washington State Ferries.

Operator & SHIP'S NAME	TONS	ELEV	H/C TOILET	PAX	CARS
BLACK BALL TRANSPORT, INC., 10777 Main St., Bellevue, WA 98004					
COHO	5315	YES	YES	750	110
Crossing time from Port Angeles to Victoria 75 min					
WASHINGTON STATE FERRIES, 801 Alaskan Way, Seattle, WA 98014-1487					
CATHLAMET	2477	YES	YES	1200	100
CHELAN	2453	YES	YES	1220	100
ELWHA	2740	NO	NO	2500	160
EVERGREEN STATE	1495	YES	NO	1000	100
HYAK	2704	NO	NO	2500	160
ILLAHEE	1369	YES	YES	800	75
ISSAQUAH	2469	YES	YES	1200	100
KALEETAN	2704	NO	NO	2500	160
KITSAP	2475	YES	YES	1200	100
KITTITAS	2467	YES	YES	1200	100
KLAHOWYA	1334	NO	NO	1140	100
KLICKITAT	1431	NO	NO	800	75
NISQUALLY	1368	YES	YES	665	75
QUINAULT	1368	YES	YES	665	75
SEALTH	2453	YES	YES	1200	100
SPOKANE	3246	Gangplank	YES	200	206
TILLIKUM	1334	NO	NO	1140	100
WALLA WALLA	3246	Gangplank	YES	2000	206
YAKIMA	2704	NO	NO	2500	160

FERRY TERMINAL	BOARDING	TOILET	CROSSING TIMES
Anacortes	Ramps	YES	
Bremerton	Ramps	YES	60 min from Seattle
Clinton	Car Dk	NO	20 min from Mukelito
Colman Pier 52, Seattle	Ramps	YES	
Edmonds	Car Dk	NO	
Fauntleroy	Car Dk	NO	
Friday Harbor	Car Dk	YES	1 hr 50 min from Anacortes
Keystone	Car Dk	YES	
Kingston	Car Dk	NO	30 min from Edmonds
Lopez Island	Car Dk	NO	45 min from Anacortes
Mukelito	Car Dk	NO	
Orcas Island	Car Dk	YES	1-1/4 hr from Anacortes
Point Defiance	Car Dk	NO	Until Summer Service.
Port Townsend	Car Dk	YES	
Shaw Island	Car DK	NO	
Sidney, B.C.	Car Dk	YES	
Southworth	Car DK	YES	35 min from Fauntleroy
Tahlequah	Car Dk	NO	
Vashon Island	Car Dk	YES	15 min from Fauntleroy
Winslow	Ramps	YES	

Table 2
North Pacific Coast car ferries with handicapped facilities.
(Cabin Door Width/Sill; Bath Door Width/Sill Height)

SHIP	TONS	ELEV	TOILET	CABIN	PAX	CABIN	BATH
ALASKA MARINE HIGHWAY, P.O. Box 25535, Juneau, AK 99802-5535							
COLUMBIA	3946	YES	YES	#207	1000	36/0	33/0
MALASPINA	2928	YES	YES	#117	750	32.5/1	*33/4
MATANUSKA	3029	YES	YES	#4A	750	33/1	30.5/1
TAKU	2458	YES	YES	#7B, 10B	500	34/1	33/1
TUSTUMENA	2174	YES	YES	#101	400	33/0	24/3
BC FERRIES, 1112 Fort St., Victoria BC, V8V 4V2 CANADA (604) 386-3431							
QN of ALBERNI	5872	YES	YES	0	1415		
QN of BURNABY	4903	YES	YES	0	987		
QN of CHILLIWACK	3568	YES	YES	0	389		
QN of COQUITIAM	6551	YES	YES	0	1442		
QN of COWICHAN	6551	YES	YES	0	1466		
QN of ESQUIMALT	9304	YES	YES	0	1394		
QN of NANAIMO	4939	YES	YES	0	987		
QN of the NORTH	8889	YES	YES	#P-10	750	35/1	35/0
QN of OAK BAY	6969	YES	YES	0	1466		
QN of PRINCE RUPERT	5864	YES	YES	NONE	458		
QN of SAANICH	9302	YES	YES	0	1394		
QN of SIDNEY	3128	YES	NO	0	989		
QN of SURREY	6969	YES	YES	0	1466		
QN of TSAWWASSEN	3127	NO	YES	0	989		
QN of VANCOUVER	9357	YES	YES	0	1360		
QN of VICTORIA	9294	YES	YES	0	1360		
SPIRIT OF BC	18790	YES	YES	(4*)	1910	*Emergency only	
SPIRIT OF VANC'V'R I.	InBuild	YES	YES	TBD	TBD	Under construction	

(Other BC Ferries do not have accessible public bathrooms aboard.)

ROUTE TIMES, (hours:minutes)

Tsawwassen/Swartz Bay	1:30	Tsawwassen/Nanaimo	2:00
Swartz Bay/Fulford Harb	:35	Chemainus/Thetis Isl.	:35
Nanaimo/Horseshoe Bay	1:30	Chemainus/Kuper	:35
Horseshoe Bay/Langdale	:40	Nanaimo/Gabriola	:20
Earls Cove/Saltery Bay	:50	Horseshoe Bay/Bowen	:20
Powell River/Texada Isl.	:35	Powell River/Comox	
Buley Bay/Denman Isl.	:10	Denman Isl./Hornby Isl.	:10
Campbell River/Quadra	:10	Quadra Isl./Cortes Isl.	:45
Port Hardy/Prince Rupert	15 to 18 hrs.	(Stops once per week at Bella Bella)	
Port McNeil/Malcolm Isl.	:25	Port McNeil/Cormoran	:45
Prince Rupert/Skidegate	8:0	Skidegate/Alliford	:20

Table 3
Great Lakes, Eastern U.S., and St. Lawrence large car ferries.
(W/H is door width/ sill height in inches.)

OPERATOR, ROUTES, & SHIP'S NAME	TONS	HANDICAPPED ELEV	TOILET	CABINS (W/H)	CROSSING TIME Hrs.:Min.
LAKE MICHIGAN					
LAKE MICHIGAN CAR FERRY SERVICE; Box 708, Ludington, MI 49431 (800) 421-4243					
Manitowoc, WI-Ludington, MI;					May-Oct. 4:00
BADGER	4,244	YES	YES	4 23/0	
LAKE HURON					
ONTARIO NORTHLAND, Owen Sound, ONT, CAN (519) 376-6601, (800) 265-3163					
Tobermory, Ont., So. Baymouth, Ont.					Apr-Oct. 1:45
CHI-CHEEMAUN	6,991	YES	YES	NO	
NINDAWAYMA	3,589	YES	YES	NO	
NEW YORK STATE					
LAKE CHAMPLAIN: Three crossings from Plattsburgh, NY-Grand Isle, VT, Port Kent, NY-Burlington, VT, & Essex, NY-Charlotte, VT.					
NEW YORK CITY: Staten Island car ferry; passenger only to Ellis Isl. and Statue of Liberty.					
LONG ISLAND: Bridgeport, CT to Port Jefferson, NY (Summer only.)					
MARTHA's VINEYARD-NANTUCKET ISLAND					
WOOD's HOLE, MARTHA'S VINEYARD & NANTUCKET ISL. S.S. AUTHORITY					
P.O. Box 284, Wood's Hole, MA 02543 (508) 548-5011					
Wood's Hole-Martha's Vineyard					Yr. Round 0:45
Hyannis, MA-Nantucket Isl.					Yr. Round 2:30
EAGLE		YES	YES	NO	
NANTUCKET		YES	YES	NO	
DELAWARE RIVER ESTUARY					
CAPE MAY-LEWES FERRY, P.O. Box 827, N. Cape May, NJ 08204, (609) 886-2718					
Cape May, NJ-Lewes, DE					Yr. Round 1:10
DELAWARE, NEW JERSEY, TWIN CAPES,					
CAPE HENLOPEN & CAPE MAY		YES	YES	NO	
SAINT LAWRENCE RIVER					
SOCIETE TRAVERSIERS QUEBEC, 109 rue Dalhousie, Quebec G1K 7A1 CANADA					
Godbout, Qc-Matane, Gaspe Peninsula, Qc.		Attendant			Yr. Round 2:20
Baie Comeau, Qc. Matane, Qc.		gratis.			Yr. Round 2:20
CAMILLE MARCOUX	6,122	YES	YES	NO	
JOHN HAMILTON GRAY	11,259	YES	YES	NO	
Trois Pistoles-Les Escoumins, Qc.					May-Oct 1:30
L'HERITAGE		NO	NO	NO	
Saint Simeon, Qc-Riviere du Loup, Qc.					May-Oct.
RADISSON		NO	NO	NO	1:30
TRANS ST. LAWRENT	2,173	NO	NO	NO	1:105
Baie St. Catherine-Tadoussac, Qc.	NO		FREE		Yr. Round 0:08
Saint Joseph de la Rive-Ile aux Coudres					Yr. Round 0:15
Quebec City-Levis, Qc.	NO		NO	Attendant free	0:15
Ile d'Anticosti from Sept-Iles, Havre Saint Pierre					Summer only

Table 4

Canada's Maritime ferries with handicapped facilities; operators noted below.

FERRY LINE OPERATORS	
(1) MARINE ATLANTIC, P.O. Box 250, N. Sydney N.S. B2A 3M3 CAN.	(800) 341-7981
(2) C.T.M.A. TRAVERSIER, Qc. G0B 1B0, CAN.	(418) 986-3278
(3) NORTHUMBERLAND FERRIES, Box 634, Charlottetown, PEI, CIA 7L3	(902) 566-3831
(4) PRINCE of FUNDY CRUISES LTD., P.O. Box 4216, Port land, ME	(800) 341-7540
(5) COASTAL TRANSPORT LTD., 400 Main St., Grand Manan Isl. NB	(506) 662-3274

SHIP'S NAME & ROUTES	TONS	HANDICAPPED ELEV	w.c.	Cabins	CABIN W/H[1]	BATH W/H[1]
LABRADOR						
Lewisporte, NFLD-Goose Bay, Labrador					June-Sept	32 hrs.
Lewisporte, NFLD-Cartwright, Labrador					June-Sept	22 hrs.
Cartwright-Goose Bay, Labrador					June-Sept	10 hrs.
(1) SIR ROBERT BOND	11,197	YES	YES	#402	30/0	No en suite
(1) NORTHERN RANGER		YES	YES	#208	30/0	30/5 shwr.
NEWFOUNDLAND						
North Sydney, N.S.-Port aux Basques, NFLD					Yr. Round	5/7.5 hrs.
North Sydney, N.S.-Argentia, NFLD					Jun-Oct.	Approx. 14 hrs.
(1) CARIBOU	27,213	YES	YES	#501, 502	35/2	29/0 shwr.
(1) JOE & CLARA SMALLWOOD	27,229	YES	YES	#502, 521	34/2	34/2 shwr.
MAGDALEN ISLANDS						
Souris, PEI-Grindstone, Magdalen Isl.					Apr-Jan	5 hrs.
(2) LUCY MAUD MONTGOMERY	YES		YES			
PRINCE EDWARD ISLAND (Northumberland Strait)						
Cape Tormentine, N.B.-Borden, P.E.I.					Yr. Round	45 min./1hr.
(1) ABEGWEIT	13,483	YES	YES		None	
(1) HOLIDAY ISLAND	3,037	YES	YES	None		
(1) VACATIONLAND	3,083	YES	YES	None		
Wood Island, PEI,-Caribou, N.S. (902) 566-3838					Apr-Dec	1.25 hrs.
(3) CONFEDERATION		NO	NO			
(3) LORD SELKIRK		NO	NO	Planned new ship to		
(3) PRINCE EDWARD		YES	YES	have elevator & H/C toilet.		
(3) PRINCE NOVA		YES	YES			
NOVA SCOTIA						
Saint John, N.B.-Digby, N.S.		PRINCESS ACADIA			Yr. Round	2.5-3 hrs.
Bar Harbor, ME-Yarmouth,		BLUENOSE			Yr. Round	6-7 hrs.
(1) BLUENOSE	6,524	YES	YES	"H/C" Cabin	35/0	29/0
(1) PRINCESS ACADIA	10,051	YES	YES	None		
Portland, ME-Yarmouth, Nova Scotia					May-Oct	11 hrs.
(4) SCOTIA PRINCE	11,968	YES	YES	#316, 317	31/1	31/7 ramped
NEW BRUNSWICK						
Black's Harbor-Grand Manan Is.						1.5 hrs.
(5) GRAND MANAN V	3,831	YES	YES			

[1] "W" = Door Width; "H" = Sill Height (in inches)

Table 5
Channel and Northern European abbreviations used in text.

BRITISH ISLES & CHANNELS SERVED			NORTHERN EUROPEAN CITIES SERVED		
AMS	Amsterdam	Ned	ARH	Århus	Den
BOU	Boulogne	Fra	BER	Bergen	Nor
CAE	Caen	Fra	BOJ	Bøjden	Den
CAI	Cairnryan	Eng	COP	Copenhagen	Den
CAL	Calais	Fra	ESB	Esbjerg	Den
CHE	Cherbourg	Fra	FAN	Fanø	Den
COR	Cork	Ire	FYN	Fynshaven	Den
DIE	Dieppe	Fra	GDA	Gdansk	Pol
DOV	Dover	Eng	GED	Gedser	Den
DUB	Dublin	Ire	GOT	Gothenburg	Swed
DUN	Dunkerque	Fra	GRE	Grena	Den
DNL	Dun Laoghaire	Ire	HAL	Halsskov	Den
FLX	Felixstowe	Eng	HAM	Hamburg	Ger
FSH	Fishbourne	Bri	HLS	Helsingborg	Swe
FLU	Flushing	Ned	HLG	Helsingør	Den
FLK	Folkstone	Eng	HEL	Helsinki	Fin
GRN	Guernsey	Bri	HIR	Hirtshals	Den
HAR	Harwich	Eng	HUN	Hundestad	Den
HOL	Holyhead	Bri	KAL	Kalundborg	Den
HOO	Hook of Holland	Ned	KIE	Kiel	Ger
HUL	Hull	Eng	KIR	Kirkenes	Nor
JER	Jersey	Bri	KNU	Knudshoved	Den
LAR	Larne	N. Ire	KOL	Kolby-Kås	Den
LEH	LeHavre	Fra	KOR	Korsor	Den
LYM	Lymington	Eng	KRI	Kristianstad	Nor
NWH	New Haven	Bri	MUR	Murmansk	Rus
NCL	Newcastle	Eng	NCL	Newcastle	Eng
OST	Ostende	Bel	NYB	Nyborg	Den
PEM	Pembroke	Eng	OSL	Oslo	Nor
PLY	Plymouth	Eng	PUT	Puttgarden	Ger
POO	Poole	Eng	ROD	Rødby	Den
PTM	Portsmouth	Eng	STA	Stavanger	Nor
RAM	Ramsgate	Eng	STO	Stockholm	Swe
RSC	Roscoff	Fra	STP	St. Petersburg	Rus
ROS	Rosslare	Ire	SUN	Sundsvall	Swe
ROT	Rotterdam	Ned	TKU	Turku	Fin
SAN	Santander	Spa	TOR	Torshaven	Faroe Is.
SRK	Sark	Bri	TRV	Travemunde	Ger
SHE	Sheerness	Bri	UME	Umea	Swe
SOU	Southampton	Eng	VAS	Vaasa	Fin
STM	St. Malo	Fra	VAR	Varberg	Swe
STR	Stranraer	Bri	VES	Vestershavn	Den
SWA	Swansea	Bri	WAR	Warnemunde	Ger
VLI	Vlissingen	Ned			
WEY	Weymouth	Eng			
YAR	Yarmouth	Isle of Wight			
ZEE	Zeebrugge	Bel			

Table 6
Major British Isles ferry links (abbreviations below)

FERRY ROUTES	IRE	BRI	SPA	FRA	NED
Britain	BI/ST	See Text	BR	BR/CN EM/SL/ST EM	NS/ST/O
Channel					
Isl. of Man	IM	IM			
N. Ireland		PO/ST CN/EM			
France		BI/ST			
Ireland	BI/ST		BR/I		
Netherlands		NS/ST/O			

Ger, Den, Nor & Swe links are listed in Tables 7 and 8.

FERRY LINE OPERATORS

Abbreviation	Ferry & Their Agents
BI	B&I Ferries-Agent: Lynott Tours, Empire State Bldg., Ste. 2619 350 5th Avenue, New York, NY 10118, (800) 221-2474, FAX: (212) 695-8347
BR	Brittany Ferries, 29588 Roscoff Cedex, France (H/C facilities on NORMANDIE) Tel: 98-29-28-28 Brochure: 98-29-28-30
CN	Condor – (Hovercraft from Dover to Boulogne, 40 min, no cars) Condor Ltd., White Rock, St. Peter Port, Guernsey, UK, Tel: 99-56-42-29
C	Color Line – (See Table 7 for data)
EM	Emeraude Lines, St.Malo 35401 Cedex, France Tel: 99-40-48-40, FAX: 99-40-57-47 (SOLIDOR II has handicapped facilities)
I	Irish Ferries, (Handicapped facilities)(25% senior discount) Lynott Tours, Empire State Bldg. Ste. 2619, 350 5th Avenue, New York, NY 10118 Tel: (212) 760-0101, FAX: (212) 695-8347
IM	Isle of Man Steam Packet Co., Tel: 0624 661-661
NS	North Sea Ferries, Tel: 0482-77177
O	Olau Line (No elevators nor H/C facilities), Tel: 0795-666666
PO	P&O (All P&O Ferries have lifts & Handicapped toilets.)Tel: 05812-276
SL	Sally Lines, (22" chair on Sally STAR), 81 Picadilly, London W1V SHF Tel: 084 359 5522, 081 858 1127, FAX: 071 355 3008
SC	Scandinavian Seaways (See Table 7)
ST	Sealink/StenaLine, Charter House, Park St., Ashford, Kent TN24 8EX, Eng. Tel: 0233-64704, US Agents: British Rail Int'l. (Handicapped Facilities) 1500 Broadway, New York, NY 10036-4015, Tel: (212) 575-2667 & Thomas Ferran: 990 2nd St. Pike, Richboro, PA 18954, Tel: (800) SEALINK
SW	Swansea Cork Ferries, Tel: 0792 45 61 16
WL	Wight Link, P.O. Box 59, Portsmouth, POI 2XB, Tel: 0705-827744

CROSSING TIMES

B & I:	DUB-HOL 3.5 hr.	I:	ROS-LEH 21 hr.	SEALINK/STENA:	
	ROS-PEM 4.5 hr.		ROS-CHE 18 hr.	CHE-SOU 6-8 hr.	FOL-BOU 2 hr.
				HAR-HOO 6.5-8 hr.	NWH-DIE 4 hr.
NS:	HUL-ROT 14 hr.	EM:	STM-JER 2.5 hr.	DUN-HOL 3.5 hr.	ROS-FSH 3.5 hr.
				DOV-CAL 1.5 hr.	LAR-STR 2.5 hr.
ISLE of WIGHT (H/C facilities):		PTM-FSH 35 min.			

Table 7
Major Scandinavian ferry links between countries.
(See below for ferry line abbreviations.)

FERRY ROUTES	NORTH SEA				DEN	BALTIC SEA			
	BRI	NED	GER	NOR		SWE	FIN	POL	RUS
Britain	See Br.Islands.		C/SS	C	SS	SS			
Denmark	SS	SS	DSB	C/SS/ST*	SS/DSB	L/SS/ST		POL	
Finland			SI			Si/VK/W		POL	B
Germany	C/SS			C	DSB	ST/B	SI		B/KRI
Netherland	See Br.Islands					SS			
Norway	C		C		C/SS/ST				FFR
Poland					POL	POL	POL		
Russia			B	FFR		B	B		
Sweden	SS	SS	ST		SS/ST		Si/VK/W	POL	B

* SS to Faroe Is. Summer only.

FERRY LINE OPERATORS AND THEIR US AGENTS

	B	C	DSB	FFR	L	NCS	POL	SI	SS	ST	VK	W
Bergen Line 505 Fifth Ave. NY, NY 10016 (800) 323-7436	X	X		X		X		X	X			X
Euro Cruises 303 W. 13th St. NY, NY 10014 (800) 688-3876	X			X		X			X	X	X	
Danish State RR Faergestationsvej 5 4970 Rodby, DK Tel: 54-6050 44			X									
DFDS Seaways (USA) 655 N.W. 9th Ave. Ft. Lauderdale, FL 33309 (800) 533-3755			X						X	X		

ABBREVIATIONS

B   Baltic Express Line
C   Color Line (former Jahre/Norway Lines)
DSB   Danish State Railroad
EU   Europa Linien
FFR   Finnmark Fylkesrederi og Ruteselskaap (Kirkenes/Bergen & Murmansk)
L   Lion Ferries
NCS   Norway's Coastal Steamers
POL   Pol Ferries
SI   Silja/Finnmark Line
SS   Scandinavian Seaways
ST   Stena
VK   Viking Lines
W   Wasa Line

Table 8
Major Scandinavian North Sea ferries.

| SHIP'S NAME | Handicapped | | Handicapped Overnight Cabins (W-width;H-sill height) "en suite" | | | | Regular Routes |
	ELEV	Public Toilet	Cabin	W/H	W/H	B/Shw	
SCANDINAVIAN SEAWAYS (Den/Eng/Ger/Ned/Nor/Swe)							
DANA ANGLIA	YES	YES	1 (H-4)	38/0	33/0	Shw	GOT, ESB
HAMBURG	YES	YES	3 (I-2)	30/0	30/0	Shw	HAM, HAR
PRINCE OF	YES	YES	2 (H-4)	30/0	30/0	Shw	Assignments vary
SCANDINAVIA			& 2 (I-2)	30/0	30/0	Shw	with season.
PRINCESS OF	YES	YES	2 (H-4)	30/0	30/0	Shw	NEW, HAR,,
SCANDINAVIA			& 2 (I-2)	30/0	30/0	Shw	AMS & GOT
QUEEN OF							
SCANDINAVIA	YES	YES	10 (H-2)	30/2	30/1	Shw	TOR, OSL
KING OF							& COP.
SCANDINAVIA	YES	YES	2 (I-4)	30/0	28/1	Shw	(Step is 3.5")

(The older WINSTON CHURCHILL serving HAM/NEW/ESB, has no H/C facilities)

| SHIP'S NAME | Handicapped | | | Crossing | | | |
	ELEV	Toilet	Cabin	"en suite?"	Time	Frequency	Routes
COLOR LINE (Former Jahre & Norway Lines) (Nor/Ger/Eng)							
KRONPRINS HARALD	YES	YES	6 (A-2)	YES	19 hrs	daily	OSL-KIE
PRINSESSE RAGNHILD	YES	YES	6 (A-2)	YES	19 hrs	daily	OSL-KIE
VENUS	YES	YES	1 (A-2)	YES	21 hrs	3/wk	NEW-STA/BER
JUPITER	YES	YES	NO	NO	4 hrs	4/day	HIR-KRI
SKAGEN	YES	YES	NO	NO	4 hrs	4/day	HIR-KRI
CHRISTIAN IV	YES	YES	NO	NO	8.5 hrs	1/day	HIR-OSL

SHIP'S NAME	ELEV	Toilet	Cabin	"en suite?"	Time	Frequency	Routes
BERGEN LINE (Norway's Coastal Steamers) some cars.							
KING HARALD	YES	YES	YES (3)	YES	7 days*		BER-KIR &
MIDNATSOL	YES	YES	YES (1)	YES	5 days*		KIR-BER
NARVIK	YES	YES	YES (1)	YES	*with stops at 35		
VESTRAALEN	YES	YES	YES (1)	YES	towns & villages.		

SHIP'S NAME	ELEV	Toilet	Cabin	"en suite?"	Time	Frequency	Routes
HORJOLFUR HH CO. (Iceland)							
THORLAKSHOFN	YES	YES	YES (2)	YES	3 hrs		Vestmannaeyger to Thorlakshofn

Table 9
Denmark's major inter & intra country ferry links (DSB).

SHIP'S NAME	ELEV	Handicapped Public Toilet	Overnight Cabin	Type Ferry	Duration	Regular Routes
DSB (Denmark & Kattegat) Year round; no overnight berths.						
DRONNING INGRID	YES	YES	None	Train only	1 hr	KOR-NYB
KRONPRINS FREDERIK	YES	YES	None	Train only	1 hr	KOR-NYB
PRINS JOACHIM	YES	YES	None	Train only	1 hr	KOR-NYB
ARVEPRINS KNUD	(1)	YES	None	Car	1 hr	HAL-KNU
HEIMDAL	YES	YES	None	Car	1 hr	HAL-KNU
KNUDSHOVED	(1)	NO	None	Car	1 hr	HAL-KNU
KRAKA	YES	YES	None	Car	1 hr	HAL-KNU
ROMSO	(1)	YES	None	Car	1 hr	HAL-KNU
SPROGO	(1)	NO	None	Car	1 hr	HAL-KNU
DANMARK	YES	YES	None	Car/Train	1 hr	ROD-PUT
DRONNING MARGRETHE	YES	YES	None	Car/Train	1 hr	ROD-PUT
PRINS HENRIK	YES	YES	None	Car/Train	1 hr	ROD-PUT
LODBORG	YES	YES	None	Car	1 hr	ROD-PUT
HOLGER DANSKE	NO	YES	None	Car	2 hr	KAL-KOL
ASK	YES	YES	None	Car	3 hr	KAL-ARH
URD	YES	YES	None	Car	3 hr	KAL-ARH
PRINSESSE ANNE-MARIE	NO	NO	None	Car	25 min	HLG-HLS
PRINCSESSE ELIZABETH	NO	NO	None	Car	25 min	HLG-HLS
THYG BRAHE	YES	YES	None	Car/Train	25 min	HLG-HLS
KONG FREDERIK IX	NO	NO	None	Car/Train	2 hr	GED-WAR
NAJADEN	NO	NO	None	Car	1 hr	BOJ-FYN
ESBJERG	NO	NO	None	Car	20 min	ESB-FAN
NORDBY	NO	NO	None	Car	20 min	ESB-FAN

(1) Elevators not suitable for wheelchairs

Table 10

Major Scandinavian Ferry Links in the Baltic Sea with handicapped facilities.

		Handicapped Facilities				
		Public	Handicapped		"en suite" for H/C	Regular
SHIP'S NAME	ELEV	Toilet	Cabin	W/H	W/H B/Shw	Routes
VIKING LINE (Swe/Fin)						
AMORELLA	YES	YES	2 (A-2)	35/0	No in cabin	STO-TKU
			2 (B-2)	35/0	private facilities.	
ATHENA	YES	YES	2 (A-2)	35/0	" "	STO-MAR
CINDERELLA	YES	YES	2 (A-2)	35/0	" "	STO-HEL
DIANA II	YES	YES	1 (A-2)	35/0	" "	KAP-NLI
ISABELLA	YES	YES	2 (A-2)	35/0	" "	HEL-24 hrs
			2 (B-2)	35/0	" "	
KALYPSO	YES	YES	2 (A-2)	35/0	" "	STO-TKU
MARIELLS	YES	YES	4 (A-2)	35/0	" "	STO-HEL
OLYMPIA	YES	YES	4 (A-2)	35/0	" "	STO-HEL
ROSELLA	YES	YES	2 (A-2)	35/0	" "	KAP-NLI

(Note: the ALANDSFARJAN has stairs and no H/C facilities)

WASA LINE (Gulf of Bothnia) – (Swe/Fin)						
FENNIA	YES	YES	YES	35/1	33/2 Shwr	Across mid
WASA KING	YES	YES	YES	33/1	33/2 Shwr	Gulf of
WASA QUEEN	YES	YES	4			BOTHNIA
POLAR PRINCESS	YES	NO	YES	29/1	22/2	

ECKERO LINE (Fin/Est)						
BOTHNIA EXPRESS	YES	---	YES	29/1	22/2 ---	GRI-ECK

SILJA LINE (Swe/Fin/Ger/Est)						
SILJA SERENADE	YES	YES	12	Deck 8;same fares as in		STO-TKU
SILJA SYMPHONY	YES	YES	12	Promenade or Seaside class		STO-HEL
SILJA EUROPA	YES	YES	12	Deck 5;Seaside & Tourist I fares		STO-HEL
FINNJET	YES	YES	None			TRV-HEL
SILJA KARNEVAL	YES	YES	4	Large Silja-like cabins;"B" fares		STO-TKU
SILJA FESTIVAL	YES	YES	4	On Decks 4 & 5-inside & outside		STO-TKU
SALLY ALBATROSS	YES	YES	2	Deck 5 same price as "B" cabin		HEL-TAL

BALTIC (BERGEN) LINE (Swe/Rus/Lat)						
ILICH	YES	NO	NO		6 day cruise	STO-STP
ANNA KARENINA	YES	NO	NO		3 day cruise	STO-RIGA
KONSTANTIN SIMONOV	YES	NO	NO		4 day cruise	STO-STP

Table 11
Mediterranean car ferry operators and U.S. agents.
(See below for ferry line abbreviations.)

ROUTES	MOR	ALG	TUN	SPA	FRA	ISR	ITA	YUG	GRE	TUR	EGY
Algeria					SN						
Egypt									AD/LO		
France		SN	SN								
Greece						SB/AR	AD/ST KR/MI/VN	ST		BS	AD/LO
Israel									SB/AR		
Italy								ST	AD/KR MI/VN		
Morocco				TR							
Spain	TR										
Tunisia				SN							
Turkey							BS				
Yugoslavia									ST		

FERRY LINES & U.S. AGENTS

AD   Adriatica
Extra Value Travel, Inc., 683 S. Collier Blvd., Marco Isl., FL 33937 (813) 394-3384
AR   Arkadia
Sea Connection Center, 757 Deep Valley Dr., RHE, CA 90247 (310) 544-3551
BS   Black Sea Shipping
25 Akti Miaouli, Pireaus, GR. Tel: 411-8075
KR   Karagerogis
Sea Connection Center, 757 Deep Valley Dr., RHE, CA 90237 (310) 544-3551
LO   Louis Cr. Lines
3 Karageorgi Servias, Athens, GR. Tel: 322-7852
MR   Marlines
European Ferries Center, 250 Old Country Rd., Mineola, NY 11501 (516) 747-8880
Sea Connection Center, 757 Deep Valley Dr., RHE, CA 90247 (310) 544-3551
SN   Marseille SNCM
61 bd. de Dames, BP 807, 13222, Marseilles, Cedex 1, France Tel: 91-56-32-00
MI   Minoan
European Ferries Center, 250 Old Country Rd., Mineola, NY 11501 (516) 747-8880
SB   Stability
European Ferries Center, 250 Old Country Rd., Mineola, NY 11501 (516) 747-8880
ST   Strintzis
Sea Connection Center, 757 Deep Valley Dr., RHE, CA 90237 (310) 544-3551
TR   Trasmediterranea
Plaza Manuel Gomez Moreno s/n, 28020 Central Madrid, Spain Tel: 555-00-49
VN   Ventouris
European Ferries Center, 250 Old Country Rd., Mineola, NY 11501 (516) 747-8880

PART II
OCEAN CRUISES

Cruise ships reach every corner of the world. They range in size from palatial sized, glittering megaliners to classy, small luxury ships. Among all of these ships, large or small, super luxury or popular, are many with one or more handicapped cabins.

The largest ones are vibrant with spectacular lounges, play areas, grand ballrooms, different sounds, and a host of activities competing nonstop for your attention. Others may be more reserved and sedate with traditional afternoon teas, more formal nights, piano bars, et al.

Like private clubs, the smallest ships provide exclusive attention and an intimate atmosphere allowing casual and friendly contact with fellow passengers. The jaded and discriminating voyager alike can now join together to cruise in style off the beaten tracks. The colorful, spicy towns of the Orient and the Medieval small ports of Europe are all there to enjoy. Spoiled and pampered in comfortably luxurious surroundings, some seek the more diamond in the rough, expeditionary cruises for more adventure.

In the final analysis, each cruise line develops an identity of its own set in part by the cruise line itself, the Captain, its Hotel Manager, and by the nationality, culture, and training of the ship's officers and crew. A good Cruise Director helps.

Thus most cruisers end up picking a ship or line they like to which they return again and again into the caring arms of their temptress and her entreaties for a repeat affair. Others like to play the field, never satisfied, looking for something different, or . . . "better." For the handicapped too, either way, the choice is theirs.

CRUISING OVERVIEW

In the next few pages, the ships with handicapped cabins, the cruise lines that operate them, their home ports, itineraries and typical seasons during which they operate there, are all briefly described.

Cruise Ships with Handicapped Cabins

Less than half of one percent of the 80,000 cabins on board some 250 cruise ships in service are accessible. A limited start, but it is improving.

One fifth of them have at least one handicapped designated cabin aboard, but as noted subsequently, many of these are not wheelchair accessible. But of all the thousands of new cabins being added every year, approximately one percent of the cabins designated as handicapped, are quite accessible; the doors are wide and sills are ramped.

Ocean cruise ships with handicapped designated cabins aboard are described more fully in the Directory found at the end of this part. Some other ships without such cabins, but whose bathroom and stateroom access are more representative, or better than average, are also included in the Directory to provide a wider choice for those with some mobility.

Descriptions of good handicapped staterooms and their bathrooms are included later in the Accommodations section of Part V. Handicapped cabins will still have some type of sill or ramp into the bathroom which is generally greater than the new ADA requirements. In many older ships, 22.5" wide traveling wheelchairs are required in the handicapped cabins. Wheelchairs and their sill problems are described briefly in Appendix A.

The ships with handicapped designated cabins listed in accordance with increasing ship size, are all noted in Table 12. Access data on others without such cabins but which are also listed in the Directory are noted at the bottom of Table 12. These latter ships are suitable only for those with some mobility since the bathrooms in particular are not accessible to any ordinary type of wheelchair. The cabin entrances may be wider (but not to the bathroom), and the cabin larger. These cabins will often have remote TV controls and a few extra grab bars but are not otherwise accessible to those who can neither stand nor walk..

Table 12
Ocean cruise ships with number of handicapped cabins described in Directory.

INCREASING SIZE SHIP: SMALLEST TO LARGEST SIZED SHIP

Under 10,000 Tons

- 2 FRONTIER SPIRIT
- 4 SEABOURN PRIDE
- 4 SEABOURN SPIRIT
- 4 ROYAL VIKING QUEEN

10 to 20,000 Tons

- 6 OCEAN PEARL
- 4 RADISSON KUNGSHOLM ('95)
- 5 °CROWN MONARCH
- 1 *REGAL EMPRESS
- 2 RADISSON DIAMOND
- 2 RADISSON RUBY ('96)
- 1 *SAPPHIRE SEAS

20 to 30,000 Tons

- 4 °CROWN DYNASTY
- 4 °CROWN JEWEL
- 2 MARCO POLO
- 3 REGENT SEA
- 2 SEAWIND CROWN
- 12 *SAGAFJORD
- 44 *VISTAFJORD

30 to 40,000 Tons

- 2 MERIDIAN
- 4 ROYAL MAJESTY
- 4 *NIEUW AMSTERDAM
- 4 *NOORDAM
- 4 *CROWN ODYSSEY
- 8 COSTA ALLEGRA
- 1 EUROPA
- 4 *ROYAL VIKING SUN
- 1 *STAR/SHIP OCEANIC

40 to 50,000 Tons

- 6 DREAMWARD
- 6 WINDWARD
- 4 VIKING SERENADE
- 4 *SEAWARD
- 6 *SKY PRINCESS
- 4 *HORIZON
- 4 ZENITH
- 4 *NORDIC EMPRESS
- 4 *CRYSTAL HARMONY
- 4 CRYSTAL SYMPHONY('95)

50 to 60,000 Tons

- 6 COSTA CLASSICA
- 6 COSTA ROMANTICA
- 4 WESTERDAM*
- 6 MAASDAM ('94)
- 6 RYNDAM
- 6 STATENDAM

60 to 70,000 Tons

- 10 STAR PRINCESS
- 2 *QUEEN ELIZABETH 2

70,000 Tons and over

- 10 *CROWN PRINCESS
- 10 REGAL PRINCESS
- 20 ECSTASY
- 20 FANTASY
- 20 FASCINATION ('94)
- 20 IMAGINATION ('95)
- 20 SENSATION
- 4 MAJESTY O'THE SEAS
- 4 MONARCH O' SEAS
- 10 *NORWAY
- 12 SUN PRINCESS ('95)

NOTE: A number of above cabins may require use of a 24" wide or "traveling" wheelchair. Please see DIRECTORY for more specific limitations.

*Personally inspected and validated as accessible for those unable to stand or walk by Mr. Tom Gilbert, President of former OPT organization. (There have been name changes on some.)

°Now: "Cunard-Crown"
( ) Year of Planned Build.

Accessibility of other ships without handicapped cabins in DIRECTORY:

CELEBRATION	HOLIDAY	ROTTERDAM
CLUB MED I	INDEPENDENCE	ROYAL ODYSSEY
CONSTITUTION	ISLAND PRINCESS	ROYAL PRINCESS
DOLPHIN IV	JUBILEE	SEABREEZE
FAIR PRINCESS	PACIFIC PRINCESS	STAR/SHIP ATLANTIC
GOLDEN ODYSSEY	REGINA RENAISSANCE	STAR/SHIP MAJESTIC
GOLDEN PRINCESS	RENAISSANCE I-VIII	TROPICALE

The Cruise Lines

Some cruise lines own the vessels they operate. Others lease vessels from the owners for their own use in good times, and return them when it fades. Name changes are frequent, and cruise lines themselves are often sold or taken over.

The ships vary from deluxe, formal, and mature, to fun-loving, and casual. Some attract a Bohemian crowd. The lines try to sell adventure, fun, or glamour, or combinations of same.

Royal Caribbean Cruise Lines, the largest single brand line, focuses on the world's largest market, the Caribbean. The largest over all cruise line Carnival, also has a strong presence in the Caribbean with its own brand ships as well as the wintering ships of its Holland America Line. In the summer, Holland America transfers the bulk of her fleet to Alaska sharing the domination of that market with Princess Cruises.

Princess Cruises (the third largest overall cruise line) concentrates on the Caribbean and Mexico in the winter, then shifts many of her ships to Alaska. Appealing to both premium and popular market segments here and worldwide too, Kloster Cruises is the parent of two fine cruise lines: Royal Viking Line and Norwegian Cruise Lines.

Cunard's older grand flagship, *Queen Elizabeth 2,* and Cunard/NAC's two ships discussed later, long dominated the market for accessible accomodations. Adding Crown Cruise Lines brings other popular cruises to what some still regard as the world's premier cruise line.

The newest upper scale lines (i.e. Crystal, Diamond, Seabourn) all have good access and provide good service for the handicapped. The *Royal Majesty* and Carnival's *Fantasy* class with a large number of cabins also offer more popularly priced options for the Caribbean.

Apart from the mechanical accessibility of the ships summarized in the Directory, the cruise line operators themselves (Tables 13a, b, c, & d) strongly influence the well being and experience of handicapped passengers. Those making an especially good effort with wheelchair passengers are all first class, moderately priced or not.

Table 13a
Ocean Cruise Line Operators and ships listed in Directory.

CRUISE LINE OPERATOR	SHIP'S NAME	H/C	PAX	TONS
American Hawaiian Cruises				
550 Kearny Street, San Francisco, CA 94108	CONSTITUTION	0	798	30,090
(415) 392-9400 / (800) 765-7000	INDEPENDENCE	0	798	30,090
No handicapped cabins but friendly helping hands on this all-American ship. Fun ashore too, in Aloha land.				
Carnival Cruise Lines	CELEBRATION	0	1840	47,262
3655 NW 87 Avenue, Miami, FL 33178	FANTASY	20	2600	70,367
(305) 599-2600 / (800) 327-7373	ECSTASY	20	2600	70,367
The largest overall cruise line operator pro-	FASCINATION ('94)	20	2600	70,367
motes the "Fun Ship" image; popular with	IMAGINATION ('95)	20	2600	70,367
family groups and the younger set.	SENSATION	20	2600	70,367
	HOLIDAY	0	1794	46,052
	JUBILEE	0	1840	47,262
	TROPICALE	0	1396	36,647
	(*Mardi Gras & Carnivale* have no H/C)			
Celebrity Cruises				
5200 Blue Lagoon Drive, Miami, FL 33126	HORIZON	4	1354	46,811
(305) 262-6677 / (800) 437-3111	MERIDIAN	2	1104	30,440
Sparkling decor in Celebrity's Cruises' new	ZENITH	4	1374	47,255
ships that have good H/C cabins.				
Club Med				
40 W. 57th St., New York, NY 10019	CLUB MED I	0	425	14,745
(212) 977-2100 / (800) CLUB-MED				
Popular with Francophiles and wine lovers, but no handicapped cabins aboard.				
Costa Cruises Lines	COSTA CLASSICA	6	1300	53,700
World Trade Center, 80 SW 8th St.	COSTA ROMANTICA	6	1350	54,000
Miami, FL 33130	COSTA ALLEGRA	8	820	30,000
(305) 358-7325 / (800) 462-6782	COSTA MARINA	4	772	30,000
Italian class in food, service, and boutiques	(*Costa Riviera, Enrica & Eugenio Costa*			
makes this first-class enjoyment all the way.	have no H/C cabins)			
Crystal Cruises				
2121 Ave. of the Stars, LA, CA 90067	CRYSTAL HARMONY	4	960	49,400
(310) 785-9300 / (800) 446-6645	CRYSTAL			
Five-Star-Plus has superb service and large	SYMPHONY (In '95)	4	960	49,400
deluxe staterooms, veranda suites.				
Cunard Line				
555 5th Ave., New York, NY 10017	QUEEN ELIZABETH 2	2	1850	67,139
(212) 880-7500				
(800) 5-CUNARD / (800) 221-4770	**Cunard/NAC:**			
All 5-star ships, on this world-class cruise line	SAGAFJORD	12	589	25,147
that started it all.	VISTAFJORD	44	736	24,492

Table 13b
Ocean Cruise Line Operators and ships listed in Directory.

CRUISE LINE OPERATOR	SHIP'S NAME	H/C	PAX	TONS
Cunard-Crown Cruise Line 555 5th Ave., New York, NY 10017 (212) 880-7500 (800) 5-CUNARD / (800) 221-4770 Now joining the Cunard family of fine cruise ships, these short family cruises and more upscale new ones are all done well.	CROWN JEWEL CROWN MONARCH CROWN DYNASTY (*Cunard Countess & Princess* have cabins)	4 5 4	800 530 800	20,000 15,270 20,000 no H/C
Diamond Cruises 2875 NE 191 St., N. Miami, FL 33180 (800) 333-333 Revolutionary twin-hull style hull is most stable, spacious, and accessible for the handicapped.	RADISSON DIAMOND RADISSON KUNGSHOLM ('95) RADISSON RUBY (Planned-pending financing:)	2 4 2	354 232 354	18,400 15,000 18,400
Dolphin /(Majesty)Cruise Lines P.O. Box 019514, Miami, FL 33101-9514 (800) 222-1003 Short sun filled Caribbean cruises on smaller ships at very affordable prices; high density, but good service.	DOLPHIN IV SEABREEZE (*Ocean Breeze* has no H/C cabins)	0 0	760 832	14,776 15,483
Hapag-Lloyd Kreuzfahrten Gustav Deetjen Allee 28215 Bremen, Germany Round the world cruises on this luxury ship; helps if you speak German.	EUROPA	1	600	37,012
Holland America Line 300 Elliott Ave. West, Seattle, WA 98119 (206) 281-3535 Rated by many as the premier cruise line of all; tipping not required but friendly Indonesian service loosens you up anyway.	MAASDAM ('94) NOORDAM NIEUW AMSTERDAM ROTTERDAM RYNDAM STATENDAM WESTERDAM	6 4 4 0 6 6 4	1266 1214 1214 1070 1266 1266 1494	55,000 33,390 33,390 38,644 55,000 55,000 53,872
Lib/Go Tours 69 Spring St. Ramsey, NJ 07446 (212) 385-7680/(201) 934-3500 New England, Canada, Bahamas, and party cruises based in New York.	REGAL EMPRESS	1	875	23,000
Majesty Cruise Line 901 S. American Way, Miami FL 33132-2073 (305) 447-9660 / (800) 327-7030 Well ramped throughout on this warm teak-wooded popular ship from Miami.	ROYAL MAJESTY	4	1056	32,400

Table 13c
Ocean Cruise Line Operators and ships listed in Directory.

CRUISE LINE OPERATOR	SHIP'S NAME	H/C	PAX	TONS
Norwegian Cruise Line	DREAMWARD	6	1246	41,000
95 Merrick Way, Coral Gables, FL 33134	WINDWARD	6	1246	41,000
(305) 447-9660 / (800) 327-7030	SEAWARD	4	1534	42,276
Fine restaurants, friendly service are all stan-	NORWAY	10	2022	76,049
dard with excellent care for handicapped.	(*Southward, Starward, & Westward* have no H/C cabins)			
Orient Cruises	MARCO POLO	2	850	20,502
1510 SE 17th Street				
Ft. Lauderdale, FL 33316				
(305) 527-6660				
Larger German-built ice-hardened expedi-				
tionary cuises to Orient and Antarctica				
Pearl Cruises	OCEAN PEARL	6	483	12,476
6301 N.W. 5th Way, Ste. 4000				
Ft. Lauderdale, FL 33309				
(305) 772-8600, (800) 556-8850				
Exotic Far East cruises rated with world's				
best itineraries.				
Premier Cruise Lines	STARSHIP ATLANTIC	0	1600	30,262
P.O. Box 573, Cape Canaveral, FL 32960	STARSHIP OCEANIC	1	1100	27,645
(407) 783-5061	STARSHIP MAJESTIC	0	1027	17,503
(800) 456-1644 / (800) 888-6759				
Short Bahama cruises with tie-ins to Disney				
World make for bargain family entertainment.				
Princess Cruises	CROWN PRINCESS	10	1590	70,000
10100 Santa Monica Blvd., LA, CA 90067	REGAL PRINCESS	10	1590	70,000
(213) 553-1770	STAR PRINCESS	10	1490	63,524
(800) 421-0522 / (800) 344-2626	SUN PRINCESS ('95)	TBD	1950	77,000
Always a treat on one of these ships of P&O	SKY PRINCESS	6	1200	46,000
Lines "Love Boats" that put "Posh" in the	PACIFIC PRINCESS	0	610	20,000
dictionary.	ISLAND PRINCESS	0	610	20,000
	FAIR PRINCESS	0	830	25,000
	GOLDEN PRINCESS	0	890	28,000
	ROYAL PRINCESS	0	1200	45,000
Regency Cruises				
260 Madison Ave., New York, NY 10016				
(212) 972-4774	REGENT SEA	3	712	22,000
(800) 388-5500 / (800) 457-5566	(*Regent Star, Sun, & Rainbow* have			
Affordable rates with continental cuisine;	no H/C cabins)			
popular for traditional cruise lovers.				
Renaissance Cruises				
P.O. Box 350307, Ft. Lauderdale, FL 33335	RENAISSANCE I-IV	0	110	4,000
(800) 525-5350 / (800) 525-2450	RENAISSANCE V-VIII	0	114	4,500
Large staterooms, small ship provide luxury	(*RenaissanceVII* is now *Regina Renais-*			
accommodations to small historic ports.	*sance*)			

Table 13d
Ocean Cruise Line Operators and ships listed in Directory.

CRUISE LINE OPERATOR	SHIP'S NAME	H/C	PAX	TONS
Royal Caribbean Cruise Line 1050 Caribbean Way, Miami, FL 33132 (305) 379-2601 / (305) 539-6000 (800) 327-6700 Largest brand cruise line has excellent service and good handicapped facilities.	VIKING SERENADE NORDIC EMPRESS MAJESTY of the SEAS MONARCH of the SEAS (*Sun Viking, Song of Norway & America, Sovereign of the Seas,* and *Nordic Prince* have no H/C cabins.)	4 4 4 4	1514 2000 2354 2354	40,132 48,563 73,192 73,192
Royal Cruise Line 1 Maritime Plaza #1400, San Fran, CA 94111 (415) 956-7200 (800) 227-5628 / (800) 227-4534 Rated one of world's best; fun with hosts with lots of "opah" and "Ya'sou" from Greek crews.	ROYAL ODYSSEY GOLDEN ODYSSEY CROWN ODYSSEY	0 0 4	750 450 1052	28,000 10,500 34,250
Royal Viking Line 95 Merrick Way, Coral Gables, FL 33134 (305) 447-9660 / (800) 327-7030 Super luxury round the world or in best small ship in Kloster's top-of-the-line cruise ships.	ROYAL VIKING QUEEN ROYAL VIKING SUN	4 4	212 758	10,000 37,845
Seabourn Cruise Line 55 Francisco St., San Fran, CA 94133 (415) 391-7444 / (800) 351-9595 All suite small luxury ship that spells elegant comfort and first class service; rated best by Conde Nast Traveler readers.	SEABOURN PRIDE SEABOURN SPIRIT	4 4	204 204	9,975 9,975
Sea Fest Cruises 8751 W. Broward Blvd., #300 Plantation, FL 33323 (305) 476-9900 Low-cost, popular cruises to Bahamas on older, renovated steamship.	SAPPHIRE SEAS	1	920	18,926
Sea Quest Cruises 600 Corporate Dr., #410 Ft. Lauderdale, FL 33334 (305) 772-7552 Explorer cruises for the adventurous and young at heart . . . in a most luxurious way.	FRONTIER SPIRIT	2	164	6,700
Seawind Cruise Line 201 Sevilla Ave., #200, Coral Gables, FL 33134 (305) 520-2020 / (800) 528-8006 Large cabins, many activities keep everyone busy on these grand Caribbean luxury cruises.	SEAWIND CROWN	2	624	24,000

The Home Ports

Florida, the cruise center of the world, has over half of all the world's sailings leaving from its ports to the world's most popular destination, the Caribbean. With more than 1.5 million annual boardings, Miami is the cruise capital; Norwegian Cruise Lines, Majesty, Royal Caribbean Cruise Lines and Carnival Cruise Lines are all based there.

Most of the better cruise lines have good children's programs including Cunard, Costa, Crystal, Holland America, NCL, Princess, Royal Caribbean Cruise Lines and American Hawaiian in Hawaii. Rated the best family cruises by Family Circle magazine with its "Camp Carnival" program for the young, Carnival now bases the *Carnivale, Mardi Gras, Ecstasy,* and *Fantasy* in fast growing Port Canaveral with Cape Kennedy and Disney World's Orlando nearby. There too, two of Premier Lines "Big Red Boats" have fun-filled activities for the younger set and great package tie-ins with Disney World as the "Official Cruise Line of Disney World."

No handicapped cabins aboard, but Dolphin Cruises also targets the family market with its purchase and refurbishment of the old *Azure Seas* into the *Ocean Breeze* and adding more family and children's playrooms in its new role as the "Official Cruise Line of Hanna-Barbera®". The Jetsons®, Yogi Bear®, and the Flintstones® now compete with Mickey and his friends. Dolphin's affiliated Majesty Cruises' *Royal Majesty* however, does have particularly good handicapped staterooms and facilities and is exceptionally well ramped throughout as a more attractive host to Hanna-Barbera®'s characters.

Table 14 lists other popular ports. Fort Lauderdale's deep-water Port Everglades, with a million boardings, is the second largest cruise ship port and is home to many ships with handicapped facilities. Princess' *Regal Princess* and Celebrity's *Zenith* as well as Cunard's Caribbean cruises are based there. Premier Line's third "Big Red Boat." is based here as are three of Holland America's ships and two Seabourn ships in the winter.

Elsewhere, Tampa is expanding its port terminals eyeing Mexico, the Western Caribbean, and eventually Cuba. St. Petersburg hosts a Russian

Table 14

Major cruise embarkation ports. Some ships that typically operate
from these ports, but reassignments between ports is common.

ATLANTIC, GULF & CARIBBEAN PORTS

New York: (Summer)
*CROWN DYNASTY
*CROWN JEWEL
*CROWN MONARCH
HORIZON
MERIDIAN
QUEEN ELIZABETH 2
(London too)
REGAL EMPRESS
VISTAFJORD (FL)
WESTWARD

San Juan:
COSTA CLASSICA
HORIZON
MONARCH OF THE SEAS
RADISSON DIAMOND
REGENT SUN
ROYAL VIKING SUN (SF)
SONG OF NORWAY
STAR PRINCESS
TROPICALE
STAR PRINCESS
STARWARD
VIKING SERENADE(LA, V)

*"CUNARD CROWN - - -"

Port Canaveral:
FANTASY
STAR/SHIP ATLANTIC
STAR/SHIP OCEANIC

Ft. Lauderdale:
CROWN PRINCESS
DREAMWARD
MERIDIAN
NOORDAM (V)
QE 2 (NY/London)
REGAL PRINCESS
ROTTERDAM
SAGAFJORD
SAPPHIRE SEAS
SEABOURN PRIDE
SKY PRINCESS
STAR/SHIP MAJESTIC
STATENDAM
VISTAFJORD
WESTERDAM
ZENITH

Aruba:
OCEAN BREEZE
SEAWIND CROWN

Tampa / St. Petersburg:
NIEUW AMSTERDAM (V)
REGENT SEA (V)

Miami:
CELEBRATION
COSTA ALLEGRA
COSTA ROMANTICA
DOLPHIN IV
ECSTASY
HOLIDAY
MAJESTY OF THE SEAS
NORDIC EMPRESS
NORWAY
ROYAL MAJESTY
SEA BREEZE
SEAWARD
SOVEREIGN OF THE
   SEAS
WESTWARD

Palm Beach:
*CROWN JEWEL
*CROWN MONARCH

New Orleans:
ENCHANTED SEAS

PACIFIC RIM PORTS

Honolulu:
CONSTITUTION
INDEPENDENCE

Singapore:
MARCO POLO
OCEAN PEARL

Sydney: (Winter)
CROWN MONARCH

San Diego / Los Angeles:
CROWN ODYSSEY
CROWN PRINCESS
JUBILEE
SOUTHWARD
STARWARD
SUN VIKING
VIKING SERENADE

San Francisco:
ROYAL VIKING SUN

Vancouver: (Summer)
CROWN PRINCESS
GOLDEN ODYSSEY
NIEUW AMSTERDAM
NOORDAM
REGAL PRINCESS
REGENT SEA
ROTTERDAM
SAGAFJORD
SKY PRINCESS
STAR PRINCESS
SUN VIKING
VIKING SERENADE
WESTERDAM

ship (naturally), while further west, New Orleans bides their time for an eventual opening up of Cuba. Further east, San Juan serves as a hub for many ships while some lines base some of their fleet as distant as Aruba.

Entrenched in New York since before the days of flight, Cunard still has a strong presence there. The *QE 2* operates between there and London in the summer after her winter world cruises. Cunard-Crown Cruises' *Crown Jewel* and *Crown Monarch* are home here in the summer too before the *Crown Jewel* returns to her Palm Beach, Florida winter home in the fall, while the *Crown Monarch* moves to the growing popular base of Sydney a half globe away. The *Regal Empress,* operated by LibGo Tours, now also uses New York as a base for its few-day, nearby trips.

In the West, Vancouver is the base of some 20 ships during Alaska's summer cruise season. Many of Princess' Caribbean winter ships, and four of Holland America's five ships together dominate this market.

Further south, San Diego's expanding facilities vie with those of Los Angeles (4th largest following the three big Florida ones). Never static, ships change bases to match the shifting market.

Elsewhere in the world, Venice, Italy and Piraeus are popular bases for Mediterranean cruises, while Singapore and Sydney serve as hubs for Far Eastern or Indian Ocean, and South Pacific cruises respectively.

Itineraries

Ferries mostly maintain regular service year round, but ships (like birds and their fellow whales of the sea) migrate with the seasons. Some cruising areas visited by ships with handicapped facilities are shown in Table 15. The Caribbean is very popular and attractively priced as is the Mexican Riviera. Alaska is especially popular as are the North Cape and Northern Europe in the summer. Further south, the Greek Islands in the Eastern Mediterranean and the French and Italian Rivieras along with their (and Spain's) nearby islands in the Western Mediterranean are also attractive cruise areas.

The Far East's exotic appeal has a growing popularity, but Bermuda, eastern Canada, and South America too offer different cultures and alternative experiences that are closer to home.

Table 15

Typical cruising areas of some of the ships with handicapped cabins.

SHIPS WITH W/C CABINS	WESTERN HEMISPHERE							EASTERN HEMISPHERE						
	PAC	AK	MX	PAN	C	NE	SA	AFR	MED	NOR	IND	SE	FE	AUS
COSTA ALLEGRA	X				X				X					
COSTA CLASSICA	X				X				X					
COSTA ROMANTICA	X				X				X					
*CROWN DYNASTY		X	X	X		X								
*CROWN JEWEL					X									
*CROWN MONARCH					X	X								X
CROWN ODYSSEY		X		X	X	X		X		X	X			
CROWN PRINCESS		X		X	X									
CRYSTAL HARMONY	X		X	X	X					X				
EUROPA	X	X	X	X	X	X		X	X		X	X	X	
FANTASY					X									
FRONTIER SPIRIT	X	X	X	X	X	X	X	X	X	X		X	X	X
HORIZON					X									
MAJESTY OF SEAS					X									
MERIDIAN				X	X		X							
MONARCH OF SEAS					X									
NIEUW AMSTERDAM		X	X	X	X									
NOORDAM		X	X	X	X									
NORDIC EMPRESS					X									
NORWAY					X									
OCEAN PEARL								X			X	X	X	X
QUEEN ELIZABAB. 2	X		X	X	X	X	X	X	X	X	X	X	X	X
RADISSON DIAMOND					X				X					
REGAL EMPRESS					X	X								
REGAL PRINCESS		X		X	X									
REGENT SEA		X			X									
ROYAL MAJESTY				X	X									
ROYAL VIKING SUN	X		X	X	X	X		X	X	X				
ROYAL VIKING QN				X	X	X			X	X	X			
SAGAFJORD	X	X	X	X	X	X	X	X			X	X	X	X
SEABOURN PRIDE				X	X	X	X		X	X				
SEABOURN SPIRIT									X			X	X	X
SEAWARD					X									
SKY PRINCESS		X		X	X									
STAR PRINCESS		X		X	X				X					
STARSHIP OCEANIC					X									
STATENDAM	X	X	X	X	X		X	X	X	X	X	X	X	X
VIKING SERENADE		X		X	X									
VISTAFJORD		X		X	X			X	X	X				
WESTERDAM		X	X	X	X									
ZENITH					X									

*Now "CUNARD-CROWN ---"

PAC Pacific Islands	AFR Africa & Canary Isl.
AK Alaska	MED Mediterranean
MX Mexican Riviera	NOR Northern Europe
PAN Panama Canal	IND India
C Caribbean	SE Southeast Asia
NE East & NE U.S. & Can.	FE Far East
SA South America	AUS Australia, N.Z. & S. Pacific

Most cruise lines concentrate on cruise areas they know and promote well. Several lines reach up into Bermuda (or cruise there from New York), the Colonial South, or New England and Canada for the autumn's colors.

Princess and Royal Caribbean Cruises plow the Caribbean in winter and also transit the Panama Canal to the Mexican Riviera and Alaska. Holland America, Crystal and Royal Cruises venture deep into the Pacific in winter and later wander off to Europe for the summer season.

With its wide decks, sunning platforms and built in marina, and one of the most accessible ships afloat, Diamond Cruise's *Radisson Diamond* is ideally suited for Caribbean winter cruises and the Mediterranean in the summer. But itineraries change frequently as the market dictates and the cruise lines experiment with new niche marketing strategies.

Cruising Seasons

Tables 16 & 17 indicate typical times of the year cruises are scheduled in both the Western and Eastern Hemispheres: Alaska and northern Europe in the summer, the Southern Hemisphere during the North's winters.

Favored by mild trade winds and fair weather, Hawaii and the Caribbean attract ships year round as does the Mediterranean. Trans-Canal cruises are popular year round too, but peak as ships reposition themselves between the Caribbean and Alaska in spring and fall. In fall and winter, Australia, the South Pacific, and Far East are popular.

Attractively priced repositioning cruises cross the Atlantic and Pacific in spring and fall. During the summer, the *QE 2* alone stays the course of the old ocean liners with its North Atlantic crossings, which some hook up with return Concorde trip to contrast the old and new.

Expeditionary cruises appeal to both nature lovers and truly adventurous. Like Arctic terns, the ships switch poles with the summers, while exploring fascinating spots along the way. For the better off with more time on their hands, it's around the world to escape the north's long wintry nights and chills.

Table 16
Time of year for most popular Western Hemisphere cruise areas.

PACIFIC	J	F	M	A	M	J	J	A	S	O	N	D	ATLANTIC
								X					Hudson Bay
Alaska					X	X	X	X					
							X	X					Greenland
							X	X	X	X			St. Lawrence
						X	X	X	X	X			New England
				X	X	X	X	X	X	X			Bermuda
				X	X			X	X	X			Colonial South
Mex. Riviera	X	X	X	X	X				X	X	X	X	
Hawaii	X	X	X	X	X	X	X	X	X	X	X	X	
	X	X	X	X	X	X	X	X	X	X	X	X	Caribbean
Transcanal	X	X	X	X	X					X	X	X	Transcanal
Galapagos	X	X	X	X	X	X	X	X	X	X	X	X	
	X	X										X	Amazon River
So. America	X	X	X						X	X	X	X	So. America
	X	X								X	X	X	Antarctica
World Cruise	X	X	X	X									World Cruise

World cruises illustrate well how ships shift operating times and locales throughout the year. In the North's winters, Cunard and her Cunard/NAC line, Hapag-Lloyd, Royal Viking, and Holland America encircle the globe in first-class ships with wheelchair cabins aboard.

Around the world, from LA to New York, in eighty days for the *QE 2* in '91, but 87 days in '92 for those two cities (or 100 days round trip from either New York or Fort Lauderdale). Add a week with different stops on the *Sagafjord* and the *Royal Viking Sun*. All of these five-star ships have good accessibility as later noted in the Directory. Holland America's *Rotterdam* too encircled the globe in '93, but in '94, it will be the beautiful new *Statendam* with its six, good handicapped cabins. In '94 too, Royal Cruise Line's *Royal Odyssey* will join this group of world-circling ships.

All of these first-class ships head for other waters in the spring: the *Sagafjord* to Alaska, the *Royal Viking Sun* to the North Cape and Baltic

Table 17

Time of year for most popular Eastern Hemisphere cruise areas.

FAR EAST & AUSTRALIA	J	F	M	A	M	J	J	A	S	O	N	D	EUROPE & AFRICA
						X	X	X	X				North Cape
					X	X	X	X	X				Baltic Sea
Japan			X	X	X	X	X	X					Greenland
China			X	X	X			X	X	X			
					X	X	X	X	X	X			Channel Coast
	X	X	X	X	X	X	X	X	X	X	X	X	Mediterranean
	X	X	X	X	X				X	X	X	X	Canary Islands
SE Asia	X	X	X	X	X			X	X	X	X		
South Pacific	X	X	X	X	X				X	X	X		
	X	X	X	X								X	Africa
Aus/N Zea	X	X	X										
Antarctica	X	X	X								X	X	
World Cruise	X	X	X	X									World Cruise

Sea, and the grand *QE 2* to her Atlantic crossings. The *Sagafjord* cruises Europe in the summer and later, the Colonial South and Bermuda, before voyaging north to New England and the St. Lawrence in the fall. Then it's to the Amazon near year's end. Meanwhile, the *Royal Viking Sun* takes in the autumn colors of Canada/New England and later the tropics between Los Angeles and Ft. Lauderdale through the Panama Canal.

There are good handicapped suites, deluxe staterooms, and both outside and less expensive inside cabins on these world-circling ships; the *Royal Viking Sun*'s large deluxe stateroom for example, is shown later in Part V (Figure 18).

In summary then, with many good handicapped facilities aboard a number of ships, and with that number growing, there are many choices for the physically handicapped among all types and sizes of ships, cruise line operators, and destinations.

REPRESENTATIVE SHIP TYPES AND SIZES

Many new cruise ships target niche, or specialty markets. They range from small, luxury, all-suite ships, to the very large, popularly-priced superships. This section briefly describes some of these new ships, large and small, as well as a classic design, medium-sized ship.

The ships are separated into three different size groupings: (1) the small under 20,000 ton ships with no more than a few hundred passengers, (2) medium sized ships from 20,000 to 40,000 tons, and (3), the large, over 40,000 ton ships which carry well over 1,000 passengers each. Within these three categories, five very different but highly rated ships are briefly described; all have good handicapped facilities.

In the smallest of ships, the highly regarded 6,700 ton *Frontier Spirit* is used here to describe expeditionary-type ships. Ranging the world at times, she now luxuriously cruises Pacific Rim shores joining a larger non-expeditionary charmer, the *Ocean Pearl* , that works the Western Pacific and Indian Ocean areas with good handicapped cabins aboard.

The discussion of smaller ships includes two of the most highly rated luxury ships, the 10,000 ton *Seabourn Pride* and her sistership *Seabourn Spirit.* An equally fine cruise ship, is their 5 star plus sistership, the *Royal Viking Queen* operated by Royal Viking.

Larger, medium sized vessels represent the bulk of the world's cruise fleet. Many of them are older, but were extensively renovated. The classic design, 5 star *Sagafjord* (and sistership *Vistafjord),* are used to characterize the best of these ships. In marked contrast to most older vessels which rarely have handicapped cabins, both the *Sagafjord* and the *Vistafjord* pioneered the way with many such cabins as noted subsequently.

For the largest of ships, the premier super-luxury 49,000 ton *Crystal Harmony* exemplifies the best in large luxury ships with both tub and roll-in shower for the handicapped. Still larger, the 71,800 ton *Crown Princess* and *Regal Princess* are used here to illustrate the largest ships with superb handicapped accommodations.

THE CLASSY SMALL SHIPS – (20,000 TONS AND UNDER)

Table 18 lists the under 20,000 ton ships that have handicapped cabins. Also included are some others without handicapped designated cabins but whose limiting factors are described in the Directory of Ships at the end of this chapter.

Many older and smaller ocean cruise ships with few decks (and correspondingly no elevators), generally have no adequate handicapped facilities. A number of new luxury ships introduced in the past few years however, are so equipped. The smallest of these all-suite ships offer private yacht and club like service, and cruise into the smallest of towns. Expeditionary vessels visit even more remote shores and smaller towns.

Expeditionary Cruises

Expeditionary cruises visit the most pristine regions of the world; both the Western and Eastern Hemisphere's coasts of Antarctica, deep into the tropical rivers of South America, up north to explore Hudson Bay and even hazard the long sought Northwest Passage, thus joining the small handful who ever made it through. The worlds of Charles Darwin, Abel Tasman, Louis Bougainville, Captain Cook, Jacques Cartier, Henry Hudson, Robert Scott, Roald Amundsen, and Admiral Byrd are all there as virginal today as they were then.

Winner of the 1991 Travel & Leisure "Mark of Innovation Award," the Super Ice-Class rated *Frontier Spirit,* is an excellent example of an expeditionary-type ship with large, accessible cabins aboard. It has a large observation lounge, single seating for meals, and over 200 square feet in its all outside, large windowed, cabin suites. Cabin numbers 409 and 411 in the plan layout shown later in Figure 5 (p. 60) are accessible with roll-in showers and bath. Two roomy elevators provide access to the boat, promenade, or sun decks.

Other non-handicapped cabins aboard ship are not accessible to the average wheelchair person. For example, the two very roomy suites on

Table 18

The smallest, under-20,000-ton ships. (100 to 1000 passengers)

SHIP	H/C CABINS	TONS	PASS	CREW	YEAR BLT/RNV	OPERATOR
CLUB MED I	*	14745	425	183	89	Club Med
CROWN MONARCH	5	15270	530	200	90	Crown Cruises.
DOLPHIN IV	*	8854	562	280	56/73	Dolphin
FRONTIER SPIRIT	2	6700	164	84	90	SeaQuest
GOLDEN ODYSSEY	*	10500	450	200	74/91	Royal Cruise L.
OCEAN PEARL	6	12475	483	208	67/87	Pearl Cruises
RADISSON DIAMOND	2	18400	354	177	92	Diamond
RAD. KUNGSHOLM	4	15000	232	134	95	Radisson
RADISSON RUBY (TBD)	2	18400	354	177	(Planned)	Diamond
RENAISSANCE I to IV	*	4000	110	67	89/90	Renaissance
RENAISSANCE V to VIII	*	4500	114	72	91/92	Renaissance
ROYAL VIKING QUEEN	4	10000	212	150	92	Royal Viking
SAPPHIRE SEAS	1	18920	920	400	44/92	Sea Fest Cr.
SEABOURN PRIDE	4	9975	204	140	88	Seabourn
SEABOURN SPIRIT	4	9975	204	140	89	Seabourn
SEABREEZE	*	15483	832	350	58/85	Dolphin

*No handicapped cabins, but other accessibility limitations are noted in the Directory.

Deck 7, have 26" wide cabin entrances with less than a 1" sill, but as found on most other ships, the bathroom door is just a little over 19" wide with a 4" sill. Other cabin entrances average only 24" wide with bathroom sills over 7" high.

Chart VIII illustrates the broad range of cruises scheduled by expeditionary type ships in the '91/92 cruise season. For more than 300 years, expeditions have attempted to complete the Northwest Passage, but since the first passage in 1906, only 50 surface ships have done so. Of those, the *Frontier Spirit* completed two of the only three successful passenger ship passages ever made. And the passengers unanimously gave the ship one of the highest ratings ever presented to a cruise ship.

Naturalists and adventurers alike love these cruises. Guest lecturers and scientists provide good insight into those beautiful natural wonders. In December '93 for example, the new ice-hardened *Marco Polo* (to visit Anarctica in December '93 and encircle it in January '94) will have

---

*At 20,502 tons, the *Marco Polo* is listed in Table 19, p. 64 instead of Table 18.

Chart VIII

Expeditionary cruises roam the world. (Courtesy of Salen Lindlad Cruising)

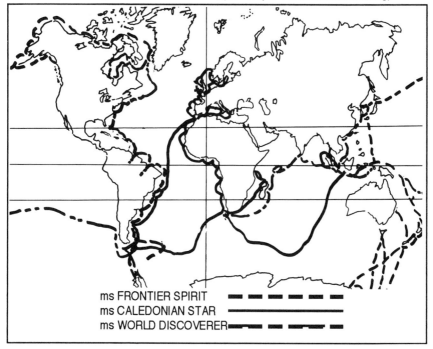

ms FRONTIER SPIRIT ▬ ▬ ▬ ▬ ▬
ms CALEDONIAN STAR ▬▬▬▬▬▬
ms WORLD DISCOVERER ▬▬ ▬ ▬▬ ▬

Antartica expert Lars-Eric Lindblad, Mt. Everest climber Sir Edmund Hillary and others of some renown aboard. Going ashore at remote landings is a problem, however. Only the physically-able can comfortably negotiate the inflatable Zodiac landing craft used to get there.

But staying aboard is not all bad. It can, in fact, be a delight. King (or queen) for a day, you have the whole ship to yourself! Read up on the early explorers from the well stocked library. You will then have a good dialog to share with the able companion who joined the shore excursion and excitedly returns brimming with the sights and wonders of their new found discoveries.

Luxury Cruises

No parkas or mosquito repellants are needed for luxury cruises. The history-steeped, picturesque cities of the world open their arms to cruise ships, large or small. But the smallest ships dock more readily in smaller

Figure 5

Handicapped cabin suites are well located on the expeditionary M/S FRONTIER SPIRIT.

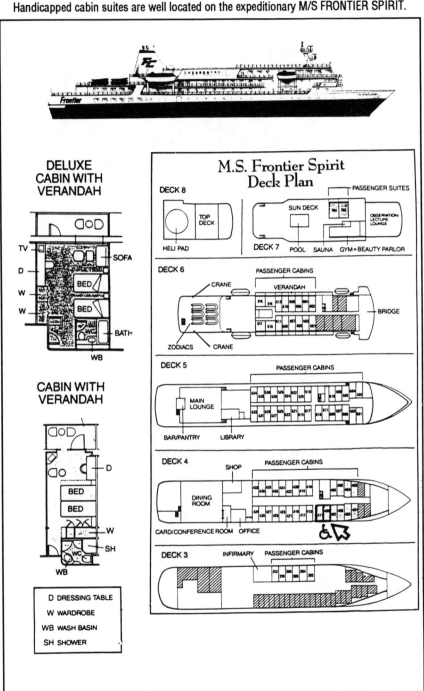

towns or sail up the rivers to moor closer to the heart of exciting cities like Bangkok, Seville, or London.

The small coastal towns reflect a taste of the region rarely experienced in the bigger ports and cites. Visit ashore without waiting in line for coffee or a glass of wine and enjoy a leisurely lunch of mussels, langouste, or bouillabaisse at a small cafe. In these towns however, some grief . . . cobblestone streets. A bumpy ride for you as you gaze enviously at local mothers pushing the smoother riding strollers with 8 large wheels over those same stones.

Fine examples of the new, all suite luxury ships are the *Seabourn Pride* and *Spirit* shown in Figure 6 with four spacious (227 sq. ft.) handicapped suites each. There are no sills into the 31" wide cabin entrance, but there is a 4" rise to the top of the sill in the 27 " wide bathroom entrance (but only a 2.5" rise from inside the "roll-in" shower floor). Four roomy elevators provide access to the upper sun and pool decks.

Not unlike the earlier discussed large car ferries, the broad stern folds down even with the water to serve as a marina for waterside activities. Other small luxury ships with built-in marinas include the *Royal Viking Queen* and the larger *Radisson Diamond* whose unique double-hulled construction is described more fully in Appendix C.

Still to come in '95, and even more luxurious, will be the *Radisson Kungsholm*. Being built at a cost of $140 million for only 116 suites, it will be the world's most spacious and expensive for the number of staterooms carried (over a million dollars per suite). Four handicapped suites are planned.

Figure 6
Luxury Ship SEABOURN PRIDE & SPIRIT Layouts.

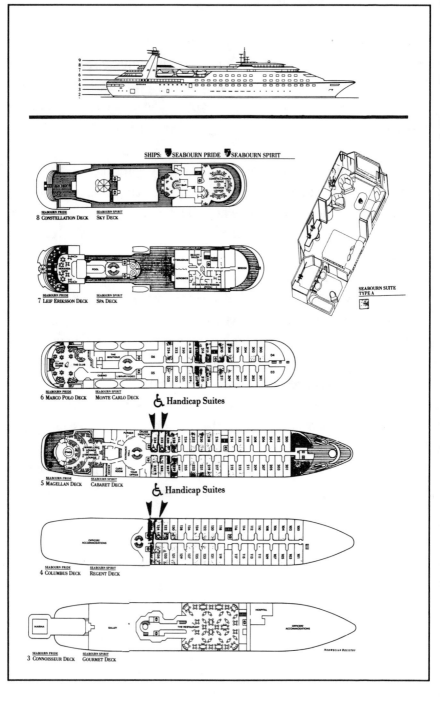

SHIPS: SEABOURN PRIDE SEABOURN SPIRIT

SEABOURN PRIDE **SEABOURN SPIRIT**
8 CONSTELLATION DECK   SKY DECK

SEABOURN PRIDE **SEABOURN SPIRIT**
7 LEIF ERIKSSON DECK   SPA DECK

SEABOURN SUITE
TYPE A

SEABOURN PRIDE **SEABOURN SPIRIT**
6 MARCO POLO DECK   MONTE CARLO DECK

Handicap Suites

SEABOURN PRIDE **SEABOURN SPIRIT**
5 MAGELLAN DECK   CABARET DECK

Handicap Suites

SEABOURN PRIDE **SEABOURN SPIRIT**
4 COLUMBUS DECK   REGENT DECK

SEABOURN PRIDE **SEABOURN SPIRIT**
3 CONNOISSEUR DECK   GOURMET DECK

NORWEGIAN REGISTRY

TRADITIONAL DESIGNS
The Bulk of the Fleet – (20,000 to 40,000)

Most of the world's cruise fleet consist of older, medium-sized vessels between 20,000 and 40,000 tons. Although many of the newer, medium-sized ships of this size (e.g., *Crown Odyssey, Nieuw Amsterdam, Noordam, Royal Viking Sun*, etc.) do have handicapped staterooms, (as do a few of the older refurbished ones noted in Table 19), the majority of ships in this size category have no such facilities aboard.

The vast majority of available handicapped cabins aboard older ships are located on just two ships: Cunard/NAC's 24,000 ton *Vistafjord* and her sistership *Sagafjord*. These ships are used to illustrate this size grouping as well as the traditional, classic ship designs developed during the great ocean liner era of centering most shipboard activities on the main or first upper deck (including the pool and sun deck aft). Newer ships follow modern design practice described earlier for the Seabourn ships and illustrated again later for the much larger *Crystal Harmony* and *Crown* and *Regal Princess*.

In silhouette, the older ships are (and were) easy to identify. Two to four large, centrally aligned stacks for larger ships. One stack vessels are pyramid shaped from the single, large, central stack with the topmost deck an unusable collection of large stacks, guys, vents, and bad air once emanating from the fire or boiler room gases of the earlier coal, or Bunker "C", oil-burning furnaces. As depicted in the layout in Figure 6 for the *Sagafjord*, this design persisted for many years, even after ships had turned to cleaner, easier to operate motor or diesel propulsion systems.

Other, older, large, steam-powered ocean liners, such as the *Norway* (ex *France* and still the largest cruise ship in the world), the *QE2* (which later converted to an electric drive system), and the *Rotterdam* which distinctively first moved its stacks aft and was one of the last steamships built, are all built along the same traditional deck layout plans as the *Sagafjord's* shown in Figures 7 and 8. It was fine service, however, that earned her the prestigious "Ship of the Year" award three different times.

Table 19
Medium sized ships listed, 20,000 to 40,000 tons. (600 to 1600 passengers)

SHIP	H/C CABINS	TONS	PASS	CREW	YEAR BLT/REN	OPERATOR
CONSTITUTION	*	30090	798	320	51/93	Am/Hawaiian
COSTA ALLEGRA	8	30000	820	374	69/92	Costa
CROWN DYNASTY	4	20000	820	300	92	Cunard-Crown
CROWN JEWEL	4	20000	820	300	92	Cunard-Crown
CROWN ODYSSEY	4	34250	1052	470	88	Royal Cruises.
EUROPA	1	37012	600	380	81	Hapag Lloyd
FAIR PRINCESS	*	25000	890	500	56/92	Princess
GOLDEN PRINCESS	*	28000	830	420	72/92	Princess
INDEPENDENCE	*	30090	798	320	50/92	Am/Hawaiian
ISLAND PRINCESS	*	20000	610	300	72	Princess
MARCO POLO	2	20502	850	450	66/93	Orient Lines
MERIDIAN	4	30440	1106	580	63/89	Celebrity
NIEUW AMSTERDAM	4	33390	1214	559	83	Holland Am.
NOORDAM	4	33390	1214	559	83	Holland Ame.
PACIFIC PRINCESS	*	20000	610	300	71	Princess
REGAL EMPRESS	1	23000	875	345	53/89	Lib/Go Tours
REGENT SEA	3	22000	712	350	57/85	Regency
ROTTERDAM	*	38644	1070	560	59/89	Holland Am.
ROYAL MAJESTY	4	32400	1056	214	92	Majesty Cr.
ROYAL ODYSSEY	*	28000	750	410	73/91	Royal Cr.
ROYAL VIKING SUN	4	37845	758	469	88	Royal Viking
SAGAFJORD	12	25147	589	352	65/83	Cunard/NAC
SEAWIND CROWN	2	24000	624	250	61/88	Seawind
STAR/SHIP ATLANTIC	*	36500	1550	500	82/88	Premier
STAR/SHIP OCEANIC	1	40000	1609	530	65/93	Premier
TROPICALE	*	36674	1396	500	81	Carnival
VISTAFJORD	44	24492	736	379	73/83	Cunard/NAC

*No handicapped cabins; other accessibility limitations noted in Directory.

A Classic Style Ship

In contrast with the newest designs, the cluttered uppermost decks of most older ships leave little room for all but an occasional sport squeezed in between the commonly found funnels, radio antennae, stays, etc.

On both the *Sagafjord* and *Vistafjord,* for example, the first usable passenger decks are the "Sun Decks" of both vessels (i.e., the Boat Decks on other vessels) where lifeboats stowed on davits stand ready for easy deployment. High sills almost always make this deck inaccessible to wheelchair passengers. With the view often blocked by the lifeboats, davits, winches etc., it is not a popular deck anyway. As on other older vessels, boat deck cabins are often large with large windows, but lifeboats and passing passengers will often block that view.

Figure 7
The SAGAFJORD's Cabin Layouts.

TERRACED OFFICERS DECK
PROMENADE DECK
VERANDA DECK
UPPER DECK
MAIN DECK
A DECK
C DECK

TERRACED SUN DECK

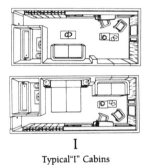

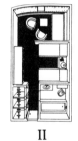

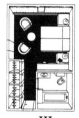

I
Typical "I" Cabins
Luxury Suites with connecting doors to transform your suite into a two-room cabin.

II
Typical "II" Cabins
Deluxe Double. Sitting area, some with private terraces and some with king-sized beds.

III
Typical "III" Cabins
Double. King-sized bed.

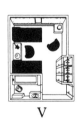

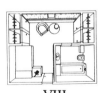

IV
Typical "IV" Cabins
Double. Two lower beds, plus one or two upper berths can be added for families.

V
Typical "V" Cabins
Double. Twin-sized beds, some of which may be converted to King-sized beds.

VI
Typical "VI" Cabins
Double. Two beds, not parallel, one of which, in some rooms, may be converted to a sofa.

VIII
Typical "VIII" Cabins
Single. Twin-sized bed.

Figure 8
The SAGAFJORD's Deck Plans.

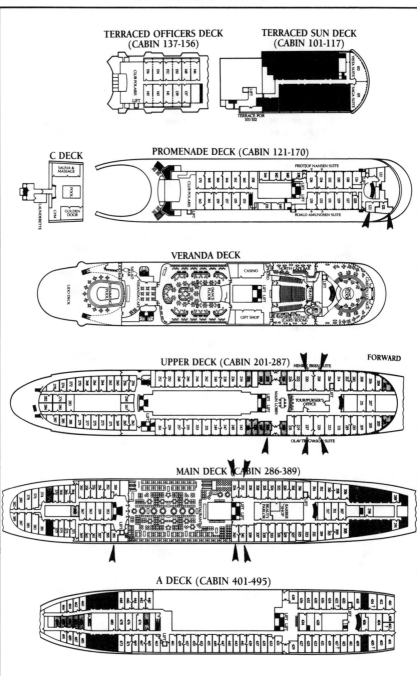

One deck below the Boat Deck is the more popular Promenade Deck (or an equivalently named alternate). With deck chairs arrayed along the side of a long covered walkway, the Promenade Deck is used by all for strolling, gazing out at the sea, reading, or just dreaming.

The Promenade Deck is used by the more able passengers for early morning jogging or walks. The long, uncluttered track encircling the ship provides ample room to stretch ones legs. But, like the Boat Deck above, it is often inaccessible to wheelchairs because of the high sill or coaming on all the topside, outward opening, watertight doors. The coamings are 8" high on the *Sagafjord* with another step or two down to the outside deck, but a small area aft of the disco (Club Polaris) is accessible. When abandoning ship, lifeboats from the Boat Deck above are lowered even with the Promenade Deck for boarding. Hopefully, many helping hands are available from crew and fellow passengers then for an assist.

Most shipboard activities are therefore centered on either the Main or first Upper Deck. Called the Veranda Deck on the *Sagafjord,* it is the first completely accessible upper deck. Lectures, games, shops, the casino, buffet, music, the library and card games, movies, entertainment, and bars or lounges are all there. Socializing or sunning is aft, around the pool.

Four elevators ("lifts" on British registry ships) provide access to most other decks. Steps block entrance to cabins on the Terraced Sun Deck, but the self-service laundry often found aboard ship is accessible on "C" Deck (but not the indoor pool and spa that are also located there).

The well-windowed, bright dining rooms of both ships provide passengers with a seaside view. At dining times however, the small elevators are often jammed with no room for a wheelchair. To avoid being the last one there, catch the empty elevator on its return trip to the top deck and be first for the return trip down.

As always, standard staterooms have high sills, but the handicapped designated cabins listed in the Directory do not. The nominal 28" cabin door, however, more typically has only a 26" clearance. Narrower still, the 26" bathroom doors in some cabins will just pass a 24" wide chair. Other bathroom doors are only 23" to 24" wide and therefore require a still narrower 22" wide traveling wheelchair.

BIG IS BEAUTIFUL   (OVER 40,000 TON MARVELS)

Megaliner Palaces. Grand and glamourous. They float? Like imagining a grand resort on "solid" earth, floating atop molten magma on one of earth's giant tectonic plates. Ships are the world's largest man-made moving objects, comparable in size to a giant skyscraper floating on its side, moving with great grandeur. An attentive staff caters to your every whim, and topside, like movie sets, a changing panorama. All of the over 40,000 ton ships listed in Table 20 with handicapped cabins are beautifully appointed, including the older, refurbished classic design *Norway* and *Queen Elizabeth 2*. The greatest increases in overall cruise capacity (along with a great increase in number of accessible accommodations) however, rest with the newest vessels.

As in most new ships, both the 49,000 ton *Crystal Harmony* and the 70,000 ton *Crown & Regal Princess* described subsequently, follow modern practice of using the two highest upper decks for the topside sunning and pool areas. The lower upper decks are more fully enclosed than in traditional designs, thereby yielding considerably more "enclosed space" for more "gross registered tonnage" in the same sized displacement vessel.

As the finest in the industry are wont to do, these ships have excellent accommodations for the handicapped. That's no surprise for Princess Cruises (the "Love Boat" line) who along with their parent P&O Line made their mark long ago as one of the finest. But it's a pleasant surprise to have the Japanese add graceful touches to every detail and luxury in the design of the *Crystal Harmony* on their first try.

A Dreamer's Delight

The most luxurious, large 5-star cruise ship *Crystal Harmony* carries less than a thousand guests in much larger than average-size staterooms (198 sq.ft. or larger). The few, smaller inside ones with 198 sq. ft. still compare favorably with the more common standard of 125 sq.ft. or less.

In common with several other grand new ships, more than half of the staterooms have private verandas including two of the 360 sq.ft. pent-

Table 20
The largest, over 40,000 ton ships. (1000 to 2600 passengers)

SHIP	H/C CABINS	TONS	PASS	CREW	YEAR BLT/REN	OPERATOR
CELEBRATION	*	47262	1840	650	87	Carnival
COSTA CLASSICA	6	53700	1300	650	92	Costa Cruises
COSTA ROMANTICA	6	54000	1350	650	93	Costa Cruises
CROWN PRINCESS	10	70000	1590	696	90	Princess
CRYSTAL HARMONY	4	49400	960	505	90	Crystal
CRYSTAL SYMPHONY	4	49400	960	505	95	Crystal
DREAMWARD	6	41000	1246	480	92	NCL
ECSTASY	20	70370	2600	980	91	Carnival
FANTASY	20	70370	2600	980	90	Carnival
FASCINATION	20	70370	2600	980	94	Carnival
HOLIDAY	*	46000	1794	714	85	Carnival
HORIZON	4	46811	1106	642	90	Celebrity
IMAGINATION	20	70370	2600	980	94	Carnival
JUBILEE	*	47262	1840	650	86	Carnival
MAASDAM	6	55000	1266	550	94	Holland Amer.
MAJESTY OF THE SEAS	4	73190	2354	780	92	RCCL
MONARCH O' THE SEAS	4	73190	2354	780	91	RCCL
NORDIC EMPRESS	4	48563	2000	686	90	RCCL
NORWAY	10	76049	2022	900	61/90	NCL
QUEEN ELIZABETH 2	2	67140	1850	1000	67/87	Cunard
REGAL PRINCESS	10	70000	1590	671	91	Princess
ROYAL PRINCESS	*	45000	1200	520	84	Princess
RYNDAM	6	55000	1266	550	93	Holland Amer.
STATENDAM	6	55000	1266	550	93	Holland Amer.
SEAWARD	4	42276	1534	630	88	NCL
SENSATION	20	70370	2600	980	93	Carnival
SKY PRINCESS	6	46000	1200	563	84	Princess
STAR PRINCESS	10	63524	1470	600	89	Princess
STATENDAM	6	55000	1266	550	92	Holland Amer.
SUN PRINCESS	TBD	77000	1950	900	95	Princess
VIKING SERENADE	4	40132	1514	614	82/91	RCCL
WESTERDAM	4	53872	1494	620	86/90	Holland Amer.
WINDWARD	6	41000	1246	480	92	NCL
ZENITH	4	47255	1374	657	92	Celebrity

*No handicapped cabins, but other accessibility limitations are noted in the Directory.

house ones equipped for the handicapped.

All four of these outside handicapped staterooms have large windows, with both bathtub and roll-in shower for the handicapped.

All decks and activities are accessible, including a long ramp to the Promenade Deck for rolling around, or in an extreme case . . . abandoning ship. As mentioned earlier, all large new ships have placed the swimming pool and a grand expanse of open sun deck on the uppermost two decks.

Enclosing most of the other upper deck regions has allowed grand multi-story atriums, a 3,000 sq. ft. duty free shopping plaza, more lounges and open deck space in addition to the larger staterooms.

Most activities are on the Tiffany Deck including a show lounge, night club, movie theatre, library, shopping area, bridge and card rooms, photo shop, and several bars. And what better place to gamble than in the Caesar's-at-Sea casino.

The handicapped staterooms are well laid out for the handicapped with wide doorways and little or no sills. Other standard staterooms follow traditional shipboard practice with 26" wide doors followed by 32" entries which it is too narrow to turn into the still narrower (22" wide) bathroom door with its formidable standard 8" high sill.

A Grand Mix

Among the largest, 70,000 ton and over ships, Carnival's popular and lively new *Fantasy* class ships have more handicapped cabins (20) than any other ship, but . . . the doors limit entrance to only narrow wheelchairs. Many families enjoy the action-packed pace and "Camp Carnival" activities for the young, but among the largest of ships, both the *Crown & Regal Princess* have the best ratio of crew members to total number of passengers and the greatest tonnage or spaciousness per passenger for a most enjoyable and comfortable cruise. Especially important are the ten large, wide-entry, and most excellent cabins for the handicapped.

Not unlike the *Crystal Harmony*, the *Crown & Regal Princess'* two uppermost Sun and Lido Decks shown in Figure 9 have large open areas for sunning, two large swimming pools and a couple of spas, with two more one deck down on the Aloha Deck. The high-domed casino, complete with dance floor and large observation windows encircling the area, is located forward on the Sun Deck.

The balcony of the large show lounge is on the boat or Dolphin Deck, together with the Library and Card Rooms. The long outside accessible walkways again are on the Promenade Deck which also has the dining room, show lounge, music room (Intermezzo), and several bars.

The beauty parlor, movie theatre, and even a top museum class, contemporary art collection are all there to attract you. There are many shops, boutiques, and saunas for some, buffets and in-pool bar for others. Still others prefer the tasty Pizzeria, the wine and caviar bar, or the patisserie for the sweeter-toothed.

As noted in the Directory at the end of this chapter, there are ten wheelchair accessible cabins: the five largest cabins are centrally located on the Dolphin Deck (four outside staterooms and one inside), and five other spacious (228 sq. ft.), inside cabins are on the Aloha Deck.

POSH it is! Coined in pre-air conditioning days a century ago by British travelers to India on Princess parent, Peninsula and Oriental (P&O) ships, it was Port Out, Starboard Home in those days for the first-class cabins. They've been that way ever since.

Figure 9
Deck plans of the grand CROWN & REGAL PRINCESS.

CROWN & REGAL PRINCESS

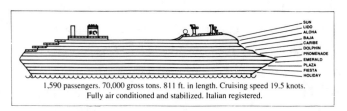

SUN
LIDO
ALOHA
BAJA
CARIBE
DOLPHIN
PROMENADE
EMERALD
PLAZA
FIESTA
HOLIDAY

1,590 passengers. 70,000 gross tons. 811 ft. in length. Cruising speed 19.5 knots.
Fully air conditioned and stabilized. Italian registered.

All first class - all with private shower and wc, refrigerator, colour television, multi-channel music system, telephones, individually controlled air-conditioning, twin beds convertible to double unless otherwise stated, walk-in dressing area.

Luxury Deluxe Suites, Outside with Verandah
Separate sitting area, bath, picture windows
A A

Deluxe Suites, Outside with Verandah
Separate sitting area, bath, picture windows
A

Deluxe Rooms, Outside with Balcony
Picture windows
B B Aloha deck
B Baja deck

Twin Rooms, Outside
Picture windows
CC Aloha deck
C Caribe deck
D EE Emerald deck
E Plaza deck
FF Plaza deck
F Dolphin deck
(safety equipment blocks view)
GG Plaza deck
(Double bed)

Staterooms
A208, A212, A216, A217, A221, & A225
have partially obstructed view.

Two berth, Outside
Upper and lower berths
G Fiesta deck

Twin Rooms, Inside
H I I Baja and Caribe decks
I Dolphin deck
J L M

FOUR BERTH STATEROOMS
● Designated staterooms will accommodate two additional people in upper berths
◆ Upper berths on Crown Princess
✗ Upper berths on Regal Princess

L Ladies Lavatories
G Gents Lavatories

SUN

LIDO

ALOHA

72

Figure 9
Deck plans of the grand CROWN & REGAL PRINCESS.

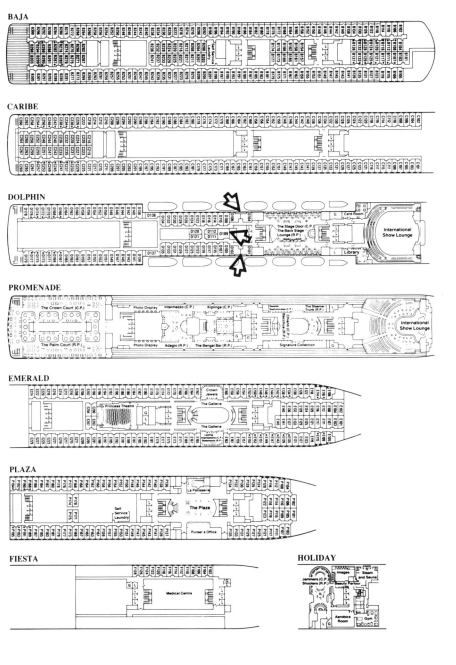

OCEAN CRUISE DIRECTORY

The following Directory includes salient data on more than 50 ocean cruise ships with handicapped designated cabins. The best cabins and limiting accessibility of 26 others without handicapped cabins per se, are also included for the convenience of those with some limited mobility.

All of these ships are listed in Table 21 arranged by total number of passengers carried with tonnage and spaciousness ratio (tons/guest) also noted. Among the ships with handicapped cabins, Table 22 lists the top 10 such ships in order of spaciousness and also by service (ratio of crew to number of guests).

The ships with an original build or service date before 1970 generally follow the classic deck plan layout described earlier for the *Sagafjord,* even if subsequently extensively refurbished (e.g., *Queen Elizabeth 2*). More recent builds, however, most often follow the modern design practice of more fully enclosing all of the upper decks to gain more "tonnage". As described earlier for the *Seabourn Pride* & *Spirit, Crystal Harmony*, and *Crown* & *Regal Princess,* the highest upper deck is generally an open sun and windscreened area with a large cut out for the large pool area one deck down.

As cautioned earlier, cruise lines must be notified of any handicap or condition before booking passage. They reserve the right to deny passage to anyone they deem to be a problem, either for the passenger himself, for fellow passengers, or as an undue burden to the cruise line itself.

The most serious barriers blocking access for persons unable to walk are generally set forth in the Directory. However, changes are frequent and, as noted earlier, passengers should revalidate any uncertainty at the time of notifying the cruise line of the particular physical, medical, or special diet restrictions they may have. Many of the cruise lines do allow powered wheelchairs, but they may limit the width to 24" chairs (as Cunard does) or the three-wheeled "Amigo"-type with gel-type batteries.* These and other wheelchairs often must also be collapsible.

* (Wet celled or acid battery types are usually banned for safety reasons.)

Table 21

Directory ships and spaciousness ratio by number of passengers carried.

PAX	SHIP' NAME	TONNAGE	TONS /PAX	PAX	SHIP'S NAME	TONNAGE	TONS /PAX
2600	ECSTASY	70,367	27	960	CRYSTAL HARMONY[2]	49,400	51
2600	FANTASY	70,367	27	TBD	CRYSTAL SYMPHONY	48,000	TBD
2600	FASCINATION	70,367	27	920	SAPPHIRE SEAS	18,826	21
2600	IMAGINATION	70,367	27	890	FAIR PRINCESS	25,000	28
2600	SENSATION	70,367	27	875	REGAL EMPRESS	23,000	26
2354	MAJESTY OF THE SEAS	73,192	31	850	MARCO POLO	20,502	24
				833	SEABREEZE	15,483	19
2354	MONARCH OF THE SEAS	73,192	31	830	GOLDEN PRINCESS	28,000	34
				820	COSTA ALLEGRA	36,000	44
2022	NORWAY	76,049	38	800	[1]CROWN JEWEL	20,000	25
2000	NORDIC EMPRESS	48,563	24	800	[1]CROWN DYNASTY	20,000	25
1950	SUN PRINCESS	77,000	39	798	CONSTITUTION	30,090	39
1850	QUEEN ELIZABETH 2	67,139	36	798	INDEPENDENCE	30,090	39
1840	CELEBRATION	47,262	26	758	ROYAL VIKING SUN	37,845	50
1840	JUBILEE	47,262	26	750	ROYAL ODYSSEY	28,000	37
1794	HOLIDAY	46,052	26	736	VISTAFJORD[2]	24,492	33
1609	STAR/SHIP OCEANIC	40,000	25	712	REGENT SEA	21,000	29
1590	CROWN PRINCESS[2]	70,000	44	624	SEAWIND CROWN	24,000	38
1590	REGAL PRINCESS[2]	70,000	44	610	ISLAND PRINCESS	20,000	33
1550	STAR/SHIP ATLANTIC	36,500	24	610	PACIFIC PRINCESS	20,000	33
1534	SEAWARD	42,276	28	600	EUROPA	37,012	62
1514	VIKING SERENADE	40,132	27	589	SAGAFJORD[2]	25,147	43
1494	WESTERDAM	53,872	36	562	DOLPHIN IV	18,845	32
1470	STAR PRINCESS	63,524	43	530	[1]CROWN MONARCH	15,270	29
1396	TROPICALE	36,674	26	483	OCEAN PEARL	12,475	25
1374	HORIZON	46,811	34	450	GOLDEN ODYSSEY	10,500	23
1374	ZENITH	47,255	34	425	CLUB MED I	14,745	35
1350	COSTA ROMANTICA	54,000	40	345	RADISSON DIAMOND	18,400	52
1300	COSTA CLASSICA	53,700	41	345	RADISSON RUBY	18,400	52
1266	MAASDAM	55,000	43	232	RADISSON KUNGSO'LM	15,000	65
1266	RYNDAM	55,000	43	212	ROYAL VIKING QUEEN	10,000	47
1266	STATENDAM	55,000	43	204	SEABOURN PRIDE[2]	9,975	49
1246	DREAMWARD	41,000	33	204	SEABOURN SPIRIT[2]	9,975	49
1246	WINDWARD	41,000	33	164	FRONTIER SPIRIT[2]	6,700	41
1214	NOORDAM	33,390	28	114	RENAISSANCE V	4,500	39
1214	NIEUW AMSTERDAM	33,390	28	114	RENAISSANCE VI	4,500	39
1200	ROYAL PRINCESS	45,000	38	114	RENAISSANCE VII	4,500	39
1200	SKY PRINCESS	46,000	38	114	RENAISSANCE VIII	4,500	39
1106	MERIDIAN	30,440	28	110	RENAISSANCE I	4,000	36
1070	ROTTERDAM	38,644	36	110	RENAISSANCE II	4,000	36
1056	ROYAL MAJESTY	32,400	31	110	RENAISSANCE III	4,000	36
1052	CROWN ODYSSEY	34,250	32	110	RENAISSANCE IV	4,000	36
1006	STAR/SHIP MAJESTIC	17,750	18				

[1]Now "CUNARD CROWN---"
[2]Deck plans in text

Table 22

The 10 best Directory ships with handicapped cabins currently in service having:
A. Highest spaciousness (tons/guest) and, B. Most service (crew/passenger) ratios.

A. SPACIOUSNESS			B. SERVICE (CREW/GUEST)		
SHIP'S NAME	H/C CABINS	TONS/ GUEST	SHIP'S NAME	H/C CABINS	CREW/ GUEST
EUROPA	1	61.7	ROYAL VIKING QUEEN	4	71%
RADISSON DIAMOND	2	53.3	SEABOURN PRIDE*	4	69%
CRYSTAL HARMONY*	4	51.5	SEABOURN SPIRIT*	4	69%
ROYAL VIKING SUN	4	49.9	ROYAL VIKING SUN	4	62%
SEABOURN PRIDE*	4	48.9	SAGAFJORD*	12	60%
SEABOURN SPIRIT*	4	48.9	STARSHIP OCEANIC	1	55%
ROYAL VIKING QUEEN	4	47.2	QUEEN ELIZABETH 2	2	54%
CROWN PRINCESS*	10	44.0	CRYSTAL HARMONY*	4	53%
REGAL PRINCESS*	10	44.0	VISTAFJORD*	44	51%
SAGAFJORD*	12	42.7	FRONTIER SPIRIT*	2	51%

*Brief description of ships are included in text as examples.

DIRECTORY

CELEBRATION
(No H/C cabins but a popular, good value ship)

OPERATIONS		SHIP		PERSONNEL	
Operator	Carnival	Tons (grt)	47,262	Passengers	1840
Flag	Bahama	Length (ft)	732	Crew	650
Trade	Caribbean	Beam (ft)	92	Nationality	
Built	1987	Draft (ft)	25	Officers	Ital
Renovated		Knots	22	Crew	Int'l

ACCESSIBILITY	OTHER	
SHIPBOARD: Step to Dining Room and sils to topside decks require assistance. No H/C public w.c.	Elevators	8
	Able Comp Req'd?	YES
HANDICAPPED CABINS: None	Power Wheelchairs?	YES
	Tendering?	YES
	with Captain's OK	

OTHER CABINS: Bathrooms not accessible due to high sil but aids are included in these larger cabins: M76 to M81, M88, M89, & M92 to M97. (i.e. large 30" cabin entry, remote TV, grab bars and shower seat.)

CLUB MED I
(No H/C cabins but popular with youthful cruisers; free table wine)

OPERATIONS		SHIP		PERSONNEL	
Operator	Club Med	Tons (grt)	14,745	Passengers	425
Flag	France	Length (ft)	614	Crew	183
Trade	Caribbean	Beam (ft)	66	Nationality	
Built	1989	Draft (ft)	16	Officers	French
Renovated		Knots	14	Crew	French

ACCESSIBILITY	OTHER	
SHIPBOARD: Only accessible to 22" wide wheelchairs with assistance. Some enjoy "gentils organisateurs" and topless.	Elevators	2
	Able Comp Req'd?	YES
HANDICAPPED CABINS: None	Tendering?	NO
	unless Captain OK's	

OTHER CABINS: Cabin entrances pass 22.5" wheelchairs, but special stool is needed in the normally inaccessible bathrooms.

CONSTITUTION

(Sistership of INDEPENDENCE; a fun cruise in Aloha land with friendly and ever helpful staff on this all American ship. One of few remaining steamships still in service.)

OPERATIONS		SHIP		PERSONNEL	
Operator	Amer. Hawaiian	Tons (grt)	30,090	Passengers	798
Flag	US	Length (ft)	682	Crew	315
Trade	Hawaii	Beam (ft)	89	Nationality	
Built	1951	Draft (ft)	30	Officers	US
Renovated	1993	Knots	20	Crew	US

ACCESSIBILITY	OTHER	
SHIPBOARD: All activities and decks are accessible except Boat and uppermost ones. Passageways are 30' wide. Ties up dockside at all ports except Kona on Big Isle.	Elevators	4
	Able Comp Req'd?	YES
	Power Chairs	YES
HANDICAPPED CABINS: None completely accessible.	Tendering?	NO

OTHER CABINS: Cabin entry 26"/2" sill; bathroom 22"/3" sill. (AA) 30/36, 33/37
   Best others: 20, 23, 24, 25, 28, 29, 18, 19, 38, 40, 41, 42, 43, 45, 84, 85, 298, 299, 16, 17, 54, 55, 14,15, 21, 22, 26, 27, 30, 31, 34,35, 39, 82, 83, 86, 87, 203, 204, 233, 234, 239, 240, 269, 274,278, 279, 56, 57, 62, 63, 68, 69, 74, 75, 80, 81, 107,.108, 113,114 119, 120, 125, 126, 131, 132, 137, 138, 151, 152, 159, 160,166,167, 172, 175, 201, 202, 207, 208, 213, 214, 219, 220, 280, 307, 309, 310, 317

COSTA ALLEGRA

(Rebuilt in 1992, the COSTA ALLEGRA has 8 H/C cabins. Converted ex container ship ANNIE JOHNSON.)

OPERATIONS		SHIP		PERSONNEL	
Operator	Costa Cr. Lines	Tons (grt)	29,500	Passengers	820
Flag	Italy	Length (ft)	614	Crew	374
Trade	Caribbean & Med	Beam (ft)	85	Nationality	
Built	1969	Draft (ft)	27	Officers	Ital
Renovated	1992	Knots	22	Crew	Int'l

ACCESSIBILITY	OTHER	
SHIPBOARD: All amenities and decks are planned accessible in recently remodeled ship. Folies Bergere, Monte Carlo casino, piano bars, etc.	Elevators	4
	Able Comp Req'd?	YES
	Tendering?	NO
HANDICAPPED CABINS: (8)	unless Captain OK's	

#3005, 3006, 3011, 3012 3013, 3014, 3019, 320
All handicapped cabins are spacious and on same deck.
All have special shower stall with fold down seat. There are no sills in handicapped cabins. Wide 33" doors to cabin and bathroom, accessible wash basin, etc.

COSTA CLASSICA
(COSTA CLASSICA's fine International cuisine and
European decor is superb along with 6 large H/C staterooms.)

OPERATIONS		SHIP		PERSONNEL	
Operator	Costa Cr. Lines	Tons (grt)	53,700	Passengers	1300
Flag	Italy	Length (ft)	723	Crew	650
Trade	Carib. & Med	Beam (ft)	98	Nationality	
Built	1992	Draft (ft)	24	Officers	Ital
Renovated		Knots	21	Crew	Int'l

ACCESSIBILITY	OTHER	
SHIPBOARD: All of the decks and activities are accessible, including public restrooms. Well appointed throughout with teak, tapestries, and original art.	Elevators (8)	YES
	Able Comp Req'd?	YES
	Power Wheelchairs?	YES
HANDICAPPED CABINS: (6)	Tendering?	NO
#4028, 4128, 5034, 6048, 6116, & 7052	(unless Captain OK's)	
All inside doubles with upper/Lower berths.		
Located on 4 separate decks: one each on Genoa and Pisa Decks, two on Amalfi & Venice Decks.No sills in handicapped cabins which have 35" wide entry door entrances to large 210 sq. ft. staterooms. Bathroom entries are 33" with fold-down shower seats.		

COSTA ROMANTICA
(Latest lovely sistership of COSTA CLASSICA serves Caribbean and Mediterranean.)

OPERATIONS		SHIP		PERSONNEL	
Operator	Costa Cr. Lines	Tons (grt)	54,000	Passengers	1350
Flag	Italy	Length (ft)	723	Crew	650
Trade	Carib. & Med	Beam (ft)	98	Nationality	
Built	1993	Draft (ft)	24	Officers	Ital
Renovated		Knots	21	Crew	Int'l

ACCESSIBILITY	OTHER	
SHIPBOARD: All of the decks and activities are accessible, including public restrooms. Well appointed throughout with teak, tapestries, and original art.	Elevators (8)	YES
	Able Comp Req'd?	YES
	Power Wheelchairs?	YES
HANDICAPPED CABINS: (6)	Tendering?	NO
#4028, 4128, 5034, 6048, 6116, & 7052	(unless Captain OK's)	
All inside doubles with upper/Lower berths.		
Located on 4 separate decks: one each on Genoa and Pisa Decks, two on Amalfi & Venice Decks.No sills in handicapped cabins which have 35" wide entry door entrances to large 210 sq. ft. staterooms. Bathroom entries are 33" with fold-down shower seats.		

CROWN ODYSSEY

(A lovely, gracious, well fitted ship with its most friendly Greek crew.)

OPERATIONS		SHIP		PERSONNEL	
Operator	Royal Cr. Line	Tons (grt)	34.250	Passengers	1052
Flag	Bahama	Length (ft)	614	Crew	470
Trade	World Wide	Beam (ft)	93	Nationality	
Built	1988	Draft (ft)	23	Officers	Greek
Renovated		Knots	22	Crew	Greek

ACCESSIBILITY	OTHER	
SHIPBOARD: All decks and activities are accessible with ramped access between public areas. Movie theatre entrance via side door of Lido Lounge to front row seats. Public bathrooms are accessible.	Elevators	4
	Able Comp Req'd?	YES
	Power Wheelchair?	YES
	Tendering?	NO
	(unless Captain OK's)	

HANDICAPPED CABINS: (4) Lido Dk. Outside doubles.
  Cat.egory CB: #8052, 8053, 8054, 8055. Cabin and bath doors: 35" with ramps over the 4" sill into bathroom withbuilt-in shower seat. "L" shaped cabin with twin beds allows full wheelchair turn circle. Tilt mirrors on vanities and bath. Toilet seat is 18.3" high. Grabbars by toilet and shower.

OTHER STANDARD CABINS: Door entry 25" wide; bathroom door 23" wide with 9" sill .

CROWN PRINCESS

(One of the latest and grandest of modern cruise ships with Princess' Cruise Lines superb service. Excellent handicapped accessibility.)

OPERATIONS		SHIP		PERSONNEL	
Operator	Princess	Tons (grt)	70,000	Passengers	1590
Flag	Liberia	Length (ft)	811	Crew	696
Trade Alaska/Pan/Caribbean		Beam (ft)	105	Nationality	
Built	1990	Draft (ft)	26	Officers	Italian
Renovated		Knots	22.5	Crew	Eur.

ACCESSIBILITY	OTHER	
SHIPBOARD: All decks are accessible, as are Casino, Theatre, Library, Lounges, Movies, Beauty Salon, Gift Shops, etc.	Elevators	9
	Able Comp Req'd?	YES
	Tendering?	YES
	(weather permitting)	

HANDICAPPED CABINS: (10) All very spacious
  doubles (228-280 sq. ft.), 33" wide doors & roll-in showers.
  Dolphin Deck: (Outside "F") #101, 103, 104, 106, (Inside "I") #109
  Aloha Deck: (Inside "H") #105, 122, 124, 125, 129.

CRYSTAL HARMONY
(Beautiful new ship with exceptionally large accessible deluxe staterooms; some suites with verandas, and H/C staterooms with bath & roll-in shower.)

OPERATIONS		SHIP		PERSONNEL	
Operator	Crystal Cruises	Tons (grt)	49,400	Passengers	960
Flag	Bahama	Length (ft)	791	Crew	505
Trade	Carib. & Europe	Beam (ft)	97	Nationality Capt.	Nor
Built	1990	Draft (ft)	25	Officers	Nor/Jap
Renovated		Knots	22	Crew	Int'l

ACCESSIBILITY

SHIPBOARD: Wide (4 ft. or more) passageways and spacious lounges and observation decks make this ultra-luxury ship a real treat for the handicapped, with all the decks accessible and well ramped.

HANDICAPPED CABINS: (4)
Beautiful large staterooms with both bath and roll-in showers.
Penthouse has private verandas.
Deluxe: (2) "E" #7108 & 7109   Penthouse: (2) "A" #1042 & 1043

OTHER STANDARD CABINS: Stateroom door widths are 26" with no sills. Bathroom door widths are 22" with 8" sills but those on Deck 10 are just 2".

OTHER

Elevators (33" to 35")	8
Able Comp Req'd?	YES
Tendering?	YES
weather permitting	

CRYSTAL SYMPHONY
(Sistership of well-ramped, super-luxury ship, CRYSTAL HARMONY will debut in '95)

HANDICAPPED CABINS: (4) Excellent large handicapped staterooms.

CUNARD CROWN DYNASTY
(Handicapped cabins on new deluxe ships have good roll-in shower bathrooms)

OPERATIONS		SHIP		PERSONNEL	
Operator	Crown	Tons (grt)	20,000	Passengers	820
Flag	Bahamas	Length (ft)	537	Crew	300
Trade Alaska/Mex/Carib/NE		Beam (ft)	74	Nationality	
Built	1993	Draft (ft)	18	Officers	N. Eur./Scand.
Renovated		Knots	18	Crew	Filipino

ACCESSIBILITY

SHIPBOARD: Well ramped throughout for access to all public areas. Public bathrooms are accessible.

HANDICAPPED CABINS: (4) Good roll-in shower bathrooms with fold down seats. Handicapped cabin and bath door openings are 32".
Deck 6: (2) #6334 & #6335 outside cabins are 200 sq.ft.
Deck 7: (2) #7118 & #7218 inside cabins are 140 sq.f.

OTHER

Elevators	6
Able Comp Req'd?	YES
Power Wheelchairs?	YES
(24" width limit)	
Tendering?	YES
(with Captain's OK)	

CUNARD CROWN JEWEL
(Crown Cruises new deluxe ships have 4 large handicapped cabins)

OPERATIONS		SHIP		PERSONNEL	
Operator	Cunard Crown	Tons (grt)	20,000	Passengers	820
Flag	Bahamas	Length (ft)	537	Crew	300
Trade	Canada/Carib.	Beam (ft)	74	Nationality	
Built	1992	Draft (ft)	18	Officers	N. Eur./Scand.
Renovated		Knots	18	Crew	Filipino

ACCESSIBILITY	OTHER	
SHIPBOARD: Well ramped throughout for access to all public areas. Public bathrooms are accessible.	Elevators	6
	Able Comp Req'd?	YES
HANDICAPPED CABINS: (4) Good roll-in shower bathrooms with fold down seats. Handicapped cabin and bath door openings are 32".	Power Wheelchairs? (24" width limit)	YES
Deck 6: (2) #6334 & #6335 outside cabins are 200 sq.ft.	Tendering? (with Captain's OK)	YES
Deck 7: (2) #7118 & #7218 inside cabins are 140 sq.ft.		

CUNARD CROWN MONARCH
(Deluxe cruise, excellent service with good range of handicapped cabins)

OPERATIONS		SHIP		PERSONNEL	
Operator	Cunard Crown	Tons (grt)	15,270	Passengers	530
Flag	Panama	Length (ft)	494	Crew	200
Trade	Canada/Carib.	Beam (ft)	69	Nationality	
Built	1990	Draft (ft)	17	Officers	N. Eur./Scand.
Renovated		Knots	18	Crew	Filipino

ACCESSIBILITY	OTHER	
SHIPBOARD: Well ramped throughout for access to all public areas. Public bathrooms are accessible.	Elevators	4
	Able Comp Req'd	YES
HANDICAPPED CABINS: (5) Spacious outside cabins with 30" doors, low sills.	Power Wheelchairs? (24" width limit)	YES
#500 (Suite),	Tendering? (with Captain's OK)	YES
#401 (Mini-suite),		
#332, 333, & 363 (Outside standard)		

DOLPHIN IV
(Smaller, higher-density, classic-type, entry- level cruises to Bahamas.)
(EX: ZION, ITHACA, AMELIA DE MELLO)

OPERATIONS		SHIP		PERSONNEL	
Operator	Dolphin Cruises	Tons (grt)	8,854	Passengers	562
Flag	Panama	Length (ft)	500	Crew	280
Trade	Bahamas	Beam (ft)	65	Nationality	
Built	1956	Draft (ft)	28	Officers	Greek
Renovated	1973	Knots	17	Crew	Int'l

ACCESSIBILITY	OTHER	
SHIPBOARD: Motorized wheelchairs allowed. Excepting Disco on Dixie Deck, aft, all other public rooms are accessible.	Elevators (26")	1
	Able Comp. Req'd?	YES
	Tendering?	YES
HANDICAPPED CABINS: None	(with Captain's OK)	
OTHER STANDARD CABINS: Cabin door width is 22", bathroom door 20". Shower sill is 3" high.		

DREAMWARD
(NCL's lovely new ship has first-rate handicapped facilities,
including staterooms for the hearing impaired. Sistership is WINDWARD.)

OPERATIONS		SHIP		PERSONNEL	
Operator	Norwegian Cr.Line	Tons (grt)	41,000	Passengers	1246
Flag	Bahama	Length (ft)	623	Crew	480
Trade	Caribbean	Beam (ft)	94	Nationality	
Built	1992	Draft (ft)	22	Officers	Nor.
Renovated		Knots	21	Crew	Int'l

ACCESSIBILITY	OTHER	
SHIPBOARD: Excepting Sky Deck, all other decks and activities are accessible. No accessible public bathrooms.	Elevators 34-36"	7
	Able Comp Req'd?	YES
HANDICAPPED CABINS: (6)	Power Wheelchairs?	YES
Handicapped cabins are well laid out with 3' wide doors & no sills to cabin and large roll-in shower bathroom in larger than standard cabins. There are special cabins for the hearing impaired too. Batteries for 3 wheel "Amigo" type power wheelchairs must be gel-celled type (no wet cell or acid type).	Tendering? unless Captain OK's	NO

Norway Deck: #8041 & 8042 are 220 sq. ft. (Outside)
Biscayne Deck: #5131 & 5132 are 198 sq. ft. (Inside)
Atlantic Deck: #6107 & 6124 are 193 sq. ft. (Inside)

ECSTASY

(Carnival's new class of high density fun ships have many H/C cabins.)

OPERATIONS		SHIP		PERSONNEL	
Operator	Carnival	Tons (grt)	70,367	Passengers	2600
Flag	Bahama	Length (ft)	856	Crew	980
Trade	Caribbean	Beam (ft)	103	Nationality	
Built	1991	Draft (ft)	26	Officers	Ital.
Renovated		Knots	21	Crew	Eur/

ACCESSIBILITY	OTHER	
SHIPBOARD: No H/C public bathrooms, some assistance required to some topside decks	Elevators	12
	Able Comp Req'd?	YES
HANDICAPPED CABINS: (20)	Power Wheelchairs?	YES
Handicapped cabins are accessible to regular 26" wide wheelchairs with 2" bathroom ramped sil. #E52, 53, 56, 57, 64 to 73, E80, 81, 116, 119, 120 & 123.	Tendering? unless Captain OK's	NO

EUROPA

(Well run, world circling and highly rated ship favored by Germans and others.)

OPERATIONS		SHIP		PERSONNEL	
Operator	Hapag Lloyd	Tons (grt)	37,012	Passengers	600
Flag	Germany	Length (ft)	654	Crew	300
Trade	World Wide	Beam (ft)	94	Nationality	
Built	1981	Draft (ft)	27	Officers	German
Renovated		Knots	21	Crew	Eur.

ACCESSIBILITY	OTHER	
SHIPBOARD: Assistance required to topside decks. Traditional decor in the most spacious of all cruise ships in tonnage per passenger.	Elevators	5
	Able Comp Req'd?	YES
	Power Wheelchairs?	YES
HANDICAPPED CABINS: (1) Spacious; ramped sill.	Tendering? unless Captain OK's	NO

FANTASY

(Carnival's new class of high density fun ships have many H/C cabins.)

OPERATIONS		SHIP		PERSONNEL	
Operator	Carnival	Tons (grt)	70,367	Passengers	2600
Flag	Bahama	Length (ft)	856	Crew	980
Trade	Caribbean	Beam (ft)	103	Nationality	
Built	1990	Draft (ft)	26	Officers	Ital.
Renovated		Knots	21	Crew	Eur/

ACCESSIBILITY	OTHER	
SHIPBOARD: No H/C public bathrooms, some assistance required to some topside decks.	Elevators	12
	Able Comp Req'd?	YES
HANDICAPPED CABINS: (20)	Power Wheelchairs?	YES
Handicapped cabins are accessible to regular 26" wide wheelchairs with 2" bathroom sill ramped. Empress Deck. #E52, 53, 56, 57, 64 to 73 E80, 81, 116, 119, 120, and 123.	Tendering? unless Captain OK's	NO

FAIR PRINCESS
(Older ship has no H.C: Ex: FAIRLAND, FAIRSEA)

OPERATIONS		SHIP		PERSONNEL	
Operator	Princess	Tons (grt)	25,000	Passengers	890
Flag	Liberia	Length (ft)	607	Crew	500
Trade	Alaska, Pan	Beam (ft)	80	Nationality	
Built	1956	Draft (ft)	29	Officers	Eur
Renovated	1972	Knots	19.5	Crew	Int'l

ACCESSIBILITY	OTHER	
SHIPBOARD: Not well suited; 4 wheelchair limit. Narrow 30" side passageways; no forward lifts on some decks.	Elevators (No fwd)	YES
	Able Comp Req'd?	YES
HANDICAPPED CABINS: NONE	Power Chairs?	YES
	Tendering? w/ Capt'n's OK	
OTHER CABINS: 22.5" cabin doors; bath 19.5" with 4" sill.		

FASCINATION
(See sistership FANTASY; planned build 1994; Trade TBD.)

HANDICAPPED CABINS (20) Planned.

FRONTIER SPIRIT
(Highly rated expeditionary ship; super ice-hardened class rated.)

OPERATIONS		SHIP		PERSONNEL	
Operator	SeaQuest	Tons (grt)	6,700	Passengers	164
Flag	Bahama	Length (ft)	361	Crew	84
Trade	Pacific Rim	Beam (ft)	56	Nationality	
Built	1990	Draft (ft)	13	Officers	Eur.
Renovated		Knots	16	Crew	Eur.

ACCESSIBILITY	OTHER	
SHIPBOARD: Dks 4,5,6,7, & boat, sun, promenade OK.	Elevators (2)	YES
HANDICAPPED CABINS: #409, 411: spacious, no sill to roll-in shower. Cabin door/Sill: 33"/0.75", bath: 33", 4" ramp,	Able Comp Req'd?	YES
	Tendering?	NO
	Zodiacs not accessible.	
OTHER CABINS: Baths have 20" doors with 8" sills.		

GOLDEN ODYSSEY
(Partially disabled treated most graciously in this friendly, cozy ship.)

OPERATIONS		SHIP		PERSONNEL	
Operator	Royal Cr. Line	Tons (grt)	10,500	Passengers	450
Flag	Bahamas	Length (ft)	427	Crew	200
Trade	World Wide	Beam (ft)	63	Nationality	
Built	1974	Draft (ft)	17	Officers	Greek
Renovated	1991	Knots	22	Crew	Greek

ACCESSIBILITY	OTHER	
SHIPBOARD: No access to gym, movies, Bellevue bar. Good accessibilty elsewhere except to uppermost deck.	Elevators (2)	30"
	Able Comp Req'd?	YES
	Power Wheelchairs?	YES
HANDICAPPED CABINS: None	Tendering?	NO
OTHER CABINS: Entries 25" (2" sills); baths 21" (8" sills)	unless Captain OK's	

GOLDEN PRINCESS
(Former 5-star plus ROYAL VIKING SKY now refurbished fro excelent Princess service)

OPERATIONS		SHIP		PERSONNEL	
Operator	Princess	Tons (grt)	28,000	Passengers	830
Flag	Bahamas	Length (ft)	674	Crew	420
Trade	Alaska, Pan	Beam (ft)	83	Nationality	
Built	1972	Draft (ft)	24	Officers	Eur
Renovated	1992	Knots	21.5	Crew	Int'l

ACCESSIBILITY	OTHER	
SHIPBOARD: Some upper deckareas inacœessible (no lift)	Elevators (No fwd)	YES
HANDICAPPED CABINS: None	Able Comp Req'd?	YES
	Power Chairs?	YES
OTHER CABINS:Cabin and Bathroom doors: 22" wide. Best cabins: Cat. AA, A, BB, #P34, C (except P51), A110, A162, A163, B229, C400, C401, C446, C449, C450, C451, & C453.	Tendering? w/ Capt'n's OK	

HOLIDAY
(Action packed, good value, but FANTASY class has better accessibilty.)

OPERATIONS		SHIP		PERSONNEL	
Operator	Carnival	Tons (grt)	46,052	Passengers	1794
Flag	Bahamas	Length (ft)	727	Crew	714
Trade	Caribbean	Beam (ft)	92	Nationality	
Built	1985	Draft (ft)	25	Officers	Ital
Renovated		Knots	21	Crew	Int'l.

ACCESSIBILITY	OTHER	
SHIPBOARD: Most public rooms accessible, but dining room has step, and there are sills to outside decks.	Elevators (2 have 30" doors)	
HANDICAPPED CABINS: None	Able Comp Req'd?	YES
	Power Wheelchairs?	YES
OTHER CABINS:Bathroom doors: 23" wide with 6" sill. Cabin entires with 30" doors: M86, 89, 90, 91, 95, 96, 97, 98, 99, & U75, 81, 85, 88.	Tendering? unless Captain OK's	NO

HORIZON
(Beautifull new ship with grandly decorated public rooms.)

OPERATIONS		SHIP		PERSONNEL	
Operator	Celebrity	Tons (grt)	46,811	Passengers	1354
Flag	Liberia	Length (ft)	682	Crew	642
Trade	Caribbean	Beam (ft)	95	Nationality	
Built	1990	Draft (ft)	24	Officers	Greek
Renovated		Knots	21.4	Crew	Int'l

ACCESSIBILITY	OTHER	
SHIPBOARD: All decks accessible, (aft elevator goes to uppermost SunDeck).	Elevators	6
	Able Comp Req'd?	YES
HANDICAPPED CABINS: (4) large outside cabins well out-fitted for handicapped; 3' plus doors wth negligible sills, roll-in shower. Europa Deck: #5048, 5049, 5060, 5061	Power wheelchairs?	YES
	Tendering? without Captain's OK	NO

IMAGINATION
(See sistership FANTASY; planned build 1995 Trade Caribbean.)

HANDICAPPED CABINS: (20)

INDEPENDENCE
(Sistership CONSTITUTION; 3-7 day Hawaiian cruises. EX; OCEANIC INDEPENDENCE)

OPERATIONS		SHIP		PERSONNEL	
Operator	Amer. Hawaiian	Tons (grt)	30,090	Passengers	798
Flag	US	Length (ft)	682	Crew	315
Trade	Hawaii	Beam (ft)	89	Nationality	
Built	1950	Draft (ft)	30	Officers	US
Renovated	1992	Knots	20	Crew	US

ACCESSIBILITY	OTHER	
SHIPBOARD: Boat and top decks are not accessible but other decks and activities are. No turn room into lower cabins with 30" wide passageways.	Elevators	4
	Able Comp Req'd?	YES
	Powered Chairs?	YES
HANDICAPPED CABINS: None	Tendering (Kona)?	NO

OTHER CABINS: Doors: cabin 26", sill 2"; bath 22", sill 3". Best others: (AA) 32/36, 33/37 Other categories: 20, 23, 24,25, 28, 29, 18, 19, 38, 40, 41, 42, 43, 45 84, 85, 16, 17, 54, 55, 14, 15, 21, 22, 26, 27, 30, 31, 34, 35, 39 82, 83, 86, 87, 203, 204 133, 134, 139, 140, 154, 260, 265, 269, 279, 56, 57, 62, 63, 68, 69, 74, 75, 80, 81, 107 108, 113, 114, 119, 120, 125, 126, 131, 132, 137, 138, 149, 150, 157, 158, 164, 165, 173, 201, 202, 207, 208, 213, 214, 219, 220, 307, 309, 310, & 317.

ISLAND PRINCESS
(Cruise Magazine's former "Ship of the Year". EX: ISLAND VENTURE)

OPERATIONS		SHIP		PERSONNEL	
Operator	Princess	Tons (grt)	19,907	Passengers	626
Flag	Great Britain	Length (ft)	554	Crew	3000
Trade	Carib./Alaska	Beam (ft)	81	Nationality	
Built	1972	Draft (ft)	24	Officers	British
Renovated		Knots	21	Cre	Eur.

ACCESSIBILITY	OTHER	
SHIPBOARD: Forward elevator only provides good access-ibility to all but Observation Deck. Short pile carpeting; one step to dining room. Limit 4 wheelchair/cruise.	Elevators	Forward
	Able Comp Req'd?	YES
	Wheelchair restrictions: 4 per cruise	
HANDICAPPED CABINS: None		

OTHER CABINS: All bathrooms have 19.5" doors, 6" sills; cabin entries vary from 22" to 33". Promenade Deck: (155 to 443 sq. ft.) #101, 102, 107, 108, 111, 112, 116, 117, 123, 124, 225, 226, 243, 244 and 346 to 350. Deluxe cabin door entries are 26.5", baths 19.5". Aloha Deck: (149 sq. ft.) #101 & 102 (141 sq. ft.) 435 & 436; 32.5" door, baths 19.5".

JUBILEE
(Bright Carnival decor, good value popular with families & the young.)

OPERATIONS		SHIP		PERSONNEL	
Operator	Carnival	Tons (grt)	47,262	Passengers	1840
Flag	Liberia	Length (ft)	732	Crew	650
Trade	Mexico	Beam (ft)	92	Nationality	
Built	1986	Draft (ft)	25	Officers	Ital.
Renovated		Knots	21	Crew	Int'l.

ACCESSIBILITY	OTHER	
SHIPBOARD: Outside decks have sills that will require assistance. Most other public rooms are accessible but Dining Room has a step. Publc bathrooms not accessible.	Elevators	8
	Able Comp Req'd?	YES
	Power Wheelchairs?	YES
HANDICAPPED CABINS: None	Tendering?	YES
	with Captain OK	

OTHER CABINS: Bathrooms have 30" door, 6" sill.
Following have enlarged cabin entry, remote TV, grab bars in bathroom, and shower stool:
Cabin#'s M76 to M81, M88, M89, and M92 to M97.

MAASDAM
(Sistership of popular STATENDAM; debuts in 1994, Trade TBD.)

HANDICAPPED CABINS: (6)

MAJESTY OF THE SEAS
(Sistership of popular SOVEREIGN OF THE SEAS and MONARCH OF THE SEAS; with good handicapped cabins)

OPERATIONS		SHIP		PERSONNEL	
Operator	Royal Caribean	Tons (grt)	73,192	Passengers	2354
Flag	Liberia	Length (ft)	880	Crew	780
Trade	Caribbean	Beam (ft)	106	Nationality	
Built	1991	Draft (ft)	25	Officers	Nor.
Renovated		Knots	21	Crew	Int'l.

ACCESSIBILITY	OTHER	
SHIPBOARD: All decks accessible with a large range of activities. wide passageways, spacious observation decks and lounges.	Elevators	YES
	Able Comp Req'd?	NO
	Powered chairs?	YES
HANDICAPPED CABINS: (4) 33" wide doors.	Tendering?	YES
	with Captain OK's	

HANDICAPPED CABINS: (4) 33" wide doors.
Category "D" (Outside Double): #9034 & 9534
Category "N" (Inside Double): #2007 & 2057
Large accessible cabins with 5' turning circles in both cabin and bath. Roll-in shower.

OTHER CABINS: Twenty other cabins have handrails etc., but with 6" to 9" sills to bath.

MARCO POLO

(Refurbished ship for $60 million has 2 cabins for H/C. Ex: Alexandr Pushkin)

OPERATIONS		SHIP		PERSONNEL	
Operator	Orient Cruises	Tons (grt)	20,500	Passengers	850
Flag	Bahamas	Length (ft)	578	Crew	450
Trade	Far East	Beam (ft)	77	Nationality	
Built	1966	Draft (ft)	27	Officers	Scand.
Renovated	1992	Knots	20	Crew	Int'l.

ACCESSIBILITY	OTHER	
HANDICAPPED CABINS: (2) Both are inside staterooms: Category H: #631 & 655	Elevators	4
	Able Comp Req'd?	YES
	Tendering?	NO
	unless Captain OK's	

MERIDIAN

(Older refurbished traditional ship. EX: GALILEO)

OPERATIONS		SHIP		PERSONNEL	
Operator	Celebrity	Tons (grt)	30,440	Passengers	1106
Flag	Bahamas	Length (ft)	700	Crew	580
Trade	Eur/Pan/N. Am.	Beam (ft)	94	Nationality	
Built	1963	Draft (ft)	29	Officers	Greek
Renovated	1989	Knots	24.5	Crew	Int'l

ACCESSIBILITY	OTHER	
SHIPBOARD: Some assist required to topside decks.	Elevators	4
HANDICAPPED CABINS: (2) Atlantic Deck #9028 & 9029 But sill in shower is inaccessible to those unable to walk.	Able Comp Req'd?	YES
	Power wheelchairs?	YES
	Tendering?	NO
	unless Captain OK's	

MONARCH OF THE SEAS

(SOVEREIGN OF THE SEAS sistership with good handicapped facilities.)

OPERATIONS		SHIP		PERSONNEL	
Operator	Royal Caribean	Tons (grt)	73,192	Passengers	2354
Flag	Liberia	Length (ft)	880	Crew	780
Trade	Caribbean	Beam (ft)	106	Nationality	
Built	1991	Draft (ft)	25	Officers	Nor.
Renovated		Knots	21	Crew	Int'l.

ACCESSIBILITY	OTHER	
SHIPBOARD: All decks accessible with a large range of activities. wide passageways, spacious observation decks and lounges.	Elevators	YES
	Able Comp Req'd?	NO
HANDICAPPED CABINS: (4)	Powered Chairs?	YES
Category "D" (Outside Double): #9034 & 9534 Category "N" (Inside Double): #2007 & 2057	Tendering?	YES
	with Captain OK's	
Large accessible cabins with 5' turning circles in cabin and bath. Roll-in shower, 33" doors.		
OTHER CABINS: Twenty other cabins have handrails etc., but with 6" to 9" sills to bath.		

NIEUW AMSTERDAM

(Good H/C facilities on always gracious, helpful Holland America ship.)

OPERATIONS	SHIP		PERSONNEL	
Operator Holland America	Tons (grt)	33,390	Passengers	1214
Flag Neth. Antilles	Length (ft)	704	Crew	559
Trade Carib./Alaska/Special	Beam (ft)	89	Nationality	
Built 1983	Draft (ft)	24	Officers	Dutch
Renovated	Knots	21	Crew	Indones/Filip

ACCESSIBILITY	OTHER	

SHIPBOARD: Excepting a few parts of some decks, all are accessible as are all activities. Handicapped public toilets. Some wheelchair rentals ($3.50/day)

HANDICAPPED CABINS: (4)
Deluxe "C" (Upper Promenade): #100, 101, 102, & 103
No sills; Cabin door 27", bathroom 34" with roll-in shower.

Elevators 31"   7
Able Comp Req'd?   NO
Power Wheelchairs?   YES
Tendering?   YES
    where practicable.

OTHER CABINS: Bathroom inaccessible but some portable commodes available.

DECK	CABIN ENTRANCE (Door W / Sill H)	BATHROOM ENTRY (Door W / Sill H)
"A" and Boat Decks:	27" / 0"	22" / 5"
Main Deck:	25" / 0"	22" / 5"

NOORDAM

(Good H/C facilities on always gracious Holland America; sistership of NIEUW AMSTERDAM)

OPERATIONS	SHIP		PERSONNEL	
Operator Holland America	Tons (grt)	33,390	Passengers	1214
Flag Neth. Antilles	Length (ft)	704	Crew	559
Trade Carib./Alaska/Special	Beam (ft)	89	Nationality	
Built 1984	Draft (ft)	24	Officers	Dutch
Renovated	Knots	21	Crew	Indones/Filip

ACCESSIBILITY	OTHER	

SHIPBOARD: Excepting a few parts of some decks, all are accessible as are all activities. Handicapped public toilets. Some wheelchair rentals ($3.50/day)

HANDICAPPED CABINS: (4)
Deluxe "C" (Upper Promenade): #100, 101, 102, & 103
No sills; Cabin door 27", bathroom 34" with roll-in shower.

Elevators 31"   7
Able Comp Req'd?   NO
Power Wheelchairs?   YES
Tendering?   YES
    where practicable.

OTHER CABINS: Bathroom inaccessible but some portable commodes available.

DECK	CABIN ENTRANCE (Door W / Sill H)	BATHROOM ENTRY (Door W / Sill H)
"A" and Boat Decks:	27" / 0"	22" / 5"
Main Deck:	25" / 0"	22" / 5"

NORDIC EMPRESS

(Good value, many amenities, and good service. Very good handicapped cabins.)

OPERATIONS		SHIP		PERSONNEL	
Operator	Royal Caribbean	Tons (grt)	48,563	Passengers	2000
Flag	Liberia	Length (ft)	692	Crew	686
Trade	Bahamas	Beam (ft)	100	Nationality	
Built	1990	Draft (ft)	23	Officers	Norw.
Renovated		Knots	20	Crew	Eur.

ACCESSIBILITY	OTHER	
SHIPBOARD: All decks are accessible as are the many activities. Wide passageways narrow down to 37" to 40" at fire doors.	Elevators –	7
	Largest 2 have 43" doors.	
	Able Comp Req'd?	NO
HANDICAPPED CABINS: (4)	Powered Chairs?	YES
Doors are 34" wide, sills are ramped to bath with roll-in shower. Full turning circles	Tendering?	YES
	with Captain's OK	
A Deck: (Inside doubles) Category "M" #4604 & 4607		
(Outside doubles) Category "M" #4548 & 4550		
OTHER CABINs:		
Cabin doors 24" but clearance is 21". Bathroom doors 20.5";sill height 6 to 9".		

NORWAY

(The largest and grandship provides lively action & good service in best classic style configuration. EX: FRANCE)

OPERATIONS		SHIP		PERSONNEL	
Operator	Norwegian Cr. L.	Tons (grt)	76,049	Passengers	2022
Flag	Bahama	Length (ft)	1035	Crew	900
Trade	Caribbean	Beam (ft)	110	Nationality	
Built	1961	Draft (ft)	33	Officers	Norway
Renovated	1990	Knots	19	Crew	Int'l.

ACCESSIBILITY	OTHER	
SHIPBOARD: All of the many activites and decks are accessible except for Uppermost Deck.Batteries for 3 wheel "Amigo" type power wheelchairs must be gel-celled (no wet cell or acid type).	Elevators 30-41"	5
	Able Comp Req'd?	YES
	Power Wheelchairs?	YES
	Tendering?	NO

HANDICAPPED CABINS: (10) Mostly with bathtubs, no "roll-in" showers; sills are 1.5".
Category 7 (Outside Double) #O-049, O-058, O-59
 Easy access from passages; 27.5" cabin door, 26.5" bathroom door.
Category 9 (Inside Double) #N-067, N-068, & P-031
 Easy access from corridor; 27.5" cabin door, 27.5" bathroom door.
Category 5 (Outside Double) #V-123, V-124, V-131, V-220
 Passageway turn limits entry to 22" wide wheelchairs.

OTHER CABINS: Cabin #I-033 entry is 27", bath 22" with 4" sill. Other shipboard cabin doorways are 22" with 1to 2" sills and bathroom doors 20" to 22" with 5" to 6" high sills.

OCEAN PEARL
(Recently renovated; rated having world's best itineraries.)
(EX: FINLANDIA, PEARL of SCANDINAVIA)

OPERATIONS		SHIP		PERSONNEL	
Operator	Pearl Cruises	Tons (grt)	12,456	Passengers	483
Flag	France	Length (ft)	517	Crew	208
Trade	Far East & Ind.	Beam (ft)	63	Nationality	
Built	1967	Draft (ft)	18	Officers	Int'l
Renovated	1987	Knots	20	Crew	Filipino

ACCESSIBILITY	OTHER

SHIPBOARD: Five inch doors on fire doors require some assistance, but decks, including uppermost Sky Deck are served by elevators.

Elevators 2
Able Comp Req'd? YES
Tendering? NO
  unless Captain OK's

HANDICAPPED CABINS: (6)

Cabin #	Cabin Door	Bathroom Door	Sill Height
701 (B)	31.5"	31.5	1.5"
612 (D)	33.5"	22.5"	3.5"
476 (E)	31.5"	24.4"	4.3"
474 (E)	33.5"	24.4"	4.3"
487 (E)	33.5"	24.4"	4.3"
489 (E)	33.5"	24.4"	4.3"

PACIFIC PRINCESS
(Good and friendly Princess Line service. Ex: SEA VENTURE)

OPERATIONS		SHIP		PERSONNEL	
Operator	Princess	Tons (grt)	19,907	Passengers	626
Flag	Great Britian	Length (ft)	554	Crew	300
Trade	Carib./Alaska	Beam (ft)	81	Nationality	
Built	1971	Draft (ft)	25	Officers	British
Renovated		Knots	21	Crew	Eur.

ACCESSIBILITY	OTHER

SHIPBOARD: All decks but Observation Deck accessible from forward elevator. One step to Dining Room. Short pile carpeting. Wheelchairs limited to 4 per cruise.

Elevators Forward ones
  accessible
Able Comp Req'd? YES
Tendering? NO
without Captain's OK

HANDICAPPED CABINS: None

OTHER CABINS:
Best of others still have 19.5" bath doors and 6" sils.
Aloha Deck: #101, 102, (149 sq. ft) and 435, 436 (141 sq. ft.) have 32.5" cabin entries.
Promenade Deck: Cabin areas range from 155 to 443 sq. ft. #101, 102, 107, 108, 111, 112, 116, 117, 123, 124, 125, 226, 243, 244, and 346-350. Deluxe Cabin entries 26.5", bath entries are 20".

QUEEN ELIZABETH 2

(A grand old 5-star classic; comfortable with most extensive renovation in history including conversion from steamship to motor vessel.)

OPERATIONS		SHIP		PERSONNEL	
Operator	Cunard	Tons (grt)	67,139	Passengers	1850
Flag	British	Length (ft)	936	Crew	1000
Trade	World Wide	Beam (ft)	105	Nationality	
Built	1967	Draft (ft)	32	Officers	Brit.
Renovated	1987	Knots	33	Crew	Eur.

ACCESSIBILITY	OTHER	
SHIPBOARD: All lower decks, Quarterdeck and Upper Deck	Elevators	13
are accessible but only cabins and the enclosed areas of	Able Comp Req'd?	YES
Boat Deck are accessible. Uppermost Sports Deck is not	Powered Chairs?	YES
accessible. Very well ramped throughout (Port Side)	Tendering?	YES
provides access to all activities and 10 of 13 Decks, but	with Captain OK	

there are steps to the Adult Center, Teen, and Yacht Clubs.
No access forward of Mauretania Restaurant. Princess Grill requires some assistance.
There are two large public handicapped toilets.

HANDICAPPED STATEROOMS: (Single cabins with no sills in cabin or bath)
   Grade UB, Deck 2: #2113 & 2120. Cabin door is 31" wide; bathroom 26".

HANDICAPPED CABINS WITH SMALL SILLS: (for 24" or less wheelchairs)
(Average Dimensions in inches: Door Width / Sill Height)

BOAT DECK:	Cabin Door 31" / 0" Bathroom 24" / 3" Step.
	8201 to 8208 Deluxe

DECK 1	Cabin Door 31" / 0"; Bathroom 26" / 3"
Grade B:	#1039, 1043, 1047, 1050, 1051, 1055, 1057

DECK 2	Cabin Door 31" / 0"; Bathroom 26" / 3"
Grade B:	#2067, 2071, 2072, 2074, 2075, 2079, 2082, 2086, 2090
Grade D:	#2059, 2098

CABINS REQUIRING PARTIAL MOBILITY TO BATHROOM:

DECK 1	Cabin Door 31" / 0"; Bathroom 26" / 3"
Grade B:	1036, 1038, 1040, 1041, 1042, 1044, 1045, 1048,
	1049, 1050, 1052, 1053, 1054
Grade C:	1028, 1030, 1031, 1033, 1060, 1062, 1063, 1064, 1065, 1067
Grade E:	1006, 1007, 1014, 1017

DECK 2	Cabin Door 31" / 0"; Bathroom 26" / 3"
(B)	2065, 2067, 2069, 2073, 2076-2078, 2080, 2083-2085, 2088, 2092
(D)	2091, 2093, 2102
(F)	2036, 2037
(UB)	2034, 2035, 2115, 2122

DECKS 3, 4, & 5	Cabin Door 36" / 0"; Bathroom 22" / 3"
(F)	3151
(G)	3145, 3148
(I)	4168, 4196
(M)	4010, 5200
(J)	3001, 3003, 3008, 3159, 3164, 4142, 4146, 4248
(L)	4014, 4042, 4044, 4204, 5084, 5166, 5168

RADISSON DIAMOND
(Revolutionary twin hull design provides exceptional stability with excellent accessibilty)

OPERATIONS		SHIP		PERSONNEL	
Operator	Diamond Cruises	Tons (grt)	18,400	Passengers	354
Flag	Finland	Length (ft)	425	Crew	177
Trade	Euro/Caribbean	Beam (ft)	105	Nationality	
Built	1992	Draft (ft)	26	Officers	Fin.
Renovated		Knots	13	Crew	Int'l.

ACCESSIBILITY	OTHER	
SHIPBOARD: Superb stability and most spacious and accessible throughout (but not to drop down marina and Beauty Salon). Wide spacious decks, no sils. Open seating in spectacular,uncrowded, dining room.	Elevators (2 very large)	3
	Able Comp Req'd?	YES
	Powered Chairs?	YES
	Tendering?	YES
	with Captain's OK	

HANDICAPPED CABINS: (2) #903 / 905 and904 / 906;
Two very spacious (234 sq.ft. each) double-deluxe outside suites (one with high sill veranda) on Deck 9. Large roll-in shower and large picture window suites. Cabin entry 34", Bath 40", 1" sill.

RADISSON KUNGSHOLM
(Most expensive andspacious super luxury yacht like vessel planned in '95)

OPERATIONS		SHIP		PERSONNEL	
Operator	Diamond Cruises	Tons (grt)	15,000	Passengers	232
Flag	Finland	Length (ft)	492	Crew	134
Trade	Medit.	Beam (ft)	69	Nationality	
Built	1995	Draft (ft)	16	Officers	Fin.
Renovated		Knots	18	Crew	Int'l.

HANDICAPPED CABINS: (4) Very spacious 320 sq.ft. suites; int'l accessibility standards.

RADISSON RUBY
(Planned sistership of RADISSON DIAMOND; Build TBD, finances being arranged.)

REGAL EMPRESS
(Popularly priced cruise ship operating out of NY. EX: CARIBE I)

OPERATIONS		SHIP		PERSONNEL	
Operator	Go Go Tours	Tons (grt)	23,000	Passengers	875
Flag	Panama	Length (ft)	612	Crew	345
Trad	N.E./Can/Bahamas	Beam (ft)	80	Nationality	
Built	1953	Draft (ft)	28	Officers	Eur/Scand
Renovated	1989	Knots	17	Crew	Int'l

ACCESSIBILITY	OTHER	
SHIPBOARD: Reasonably well ramped throughout. Also hasH/C Public bathroom.	Elevators (34")	3
	Able Comp Req'd?	YES
HANDICAPPED CABINS: (1) 22.5" chair recommended. Category 7: #P20-A, Promenade Dk; Inside double.	Power Wheelchairs?	YES
	Tendering?	YES
OTHER CABINS: Bathrooms are inaccessible	with Captain's OK	

REGAL PRINCESS

(A grand modern cruise ship, superb service, excellent handicapped accessibilty.)

OPERATIONS		SHIP		PERSONNEL	
Operator	Princess	Tons (grt)	70,000	Passengers	1590
Flag	Liberia	Length (ft)	811	Crew	696
Trade	Alaska/Caribbean	Beam (ft)	105	Nationality	
Built	1991	Draft (ft)	26	Officers	Italian
Renovated		Knots	22.5	Crew	Eur.

ACCESSIBILITY	OTHER	
SHIPBOARD: All decks accessible as are Casino, Theatre, Library, Lounges, Movies, Beauty Salon, Gift Shops, etc.	Elevators	9
	Able Comp Req'd?	YES
HANDICAPPED CABINS: (10) All very spacious doubles (228-280 sq. ft.), 33" wide doors & roll-in showers.	Tendering?	YES
	weather permitting	

(Outside "F") #101, 103, 104, 106, (Inside "I") #109, (Inside "H") #105, 122, 124, 125, 129.

REGENT SEA

(Refurbished older classic design with excellent service.)

OPERATIONS		SHIP		PERSONNEL	
Operator	Regency Cruises	Tons (grt)	22,000	Passengers	712
Flag	Panama	Length (ft)	631	Crew	350
Trade	Carib./Alaska	Beam (ft)	83	Nationality	
Built	1957	Draft (ft)	27	Officers	Greek
Renovated	1985	Knots	18	Crew	Eur.

ACCESSIBILITY	OTHER	
SHIPBOARD: Most activity areas are accessible but some require assistance as well as to topside on this older, classic design ship.	Elevators	4
	Able Comp Req'd?	YES
	Tendering?	NO
HANDICAPPED CABINS: (3)	unless Captain	
Bathroom requires limited mobility. Cabin door 29"; Bathroom 24".		

RENNAISSANCE I, II, III, IV

(Luxury small ship cruises unique areas around the world often under charter)

OPERATIONS		SHIP		PERSONNEL	
Operator	Renaissance	Tons (grt)	4,000	Passengers	114
Flag	Italy	Length (ft)	290	Crew	72
Trade		Beam (ft)	50	Nationality	
Built	1991 & 1992	Draft (ft)	12	Officers	Ital.
		Knots	18	Crew	Eur.

ACCESSIBILITY	OTHER	
SHIPBOARD: Only Uppermost Deck is not accessible. Readily provided assistance elsewhere.	Elevators	31"
	Able Comp Req'd?	YES
	Tendering?	YES
HANDICAPPED CABINS: None	with Captain's OK	
	but most often docks.	
OTHER STATEROOMS: All suite configuration: 210 to 287 sq. ft. staterooms. Cabin door entrance 33"; Bathroom door 23"/7" sill.		

RENNAISSANCE V, VI VII, VIII
(Luxury small ship cruises unique areas around the world often under charter)

Similar, but slightly larger (4500 tons) than RENAISSANCE I though IV, Often docks.

ROTTERDAM
(Grand old wonderful ship with superb Holland America service.)

OPERATIONS		SHIP		PERSONNEL	
Operator	Holland America	Tons (grt)	38,645	Passengers	1114
Flag	Netherlands	Length (ft)	749	Crew	603
Trade	Spec./Carib./Alaska	Beam (ft)	94	Nationality	
Built	1959	Draft (ft)	30	Officers	Dutch
Renovated	1991	Knots	22	Crew	Indones/Filipino

ACCESSIBILITY	OTHER	
SHIPBOARD: All decks accessible although some parts may require assistance. Some wheelchairs available for rent at $3.50/day.	Elevators 31"	8
	Able Comp Req'd?	NO
	if self sufficient.	
HANDICAPPED CABINS: None	Power Wheelchairs?	YES
	Tendering?	YES
OTHER CABINS: 23,5" bathroom doors may be removed. Ramps available for bathroom sills (5" on Main & "A" Dk;	if practicable.	

6" on "B" Dk.) Portable commodes if needed. Cabinentries 29" doors on Main & "A" Decks, 26" on "B" with 2" sills.

ROYAL MAJESTY
(Well ramped ship throughout offers attractively priced 3, 4, & 7 day cruises.)

OPERATIONS		SHIP		PERSONNEL	
Operator	Majesty Cruises	Tons (grt)	32,400	Passengers	1056
Flag	Panama	Length (ft)	569	Crew	510
Trade	Mex/Carib	Beam (ft)	91	Nationality	
Built	1992	Draft (ft)	19	Officers	Engl..
Renovated		Knots	21	Crew	Int'l.

ACCESSIBILITY	OTHER	
SHIPBOARD: Excellent accessibility; Very well ramped including to Promenade Deck. Teak and brass. No smoking in Dining Room. Handicapped public bathrooms.	Elevators	4
	Able Comp Req'd?	YES
	Power Wheelchairs?	YES
	Tendering?	NO
HANDICAPPED CABINS: (4) #730, 734, 735, 739	unless Captain OK's	
Four handicapped cabins with good accessibility. Door 36" & 30". Handicapped cabin can accommodate 3rd person.		

ROYAL ODYSSEY
(Royal Cruise Line's newly refurbished 5-star ship. EX: ROYAL VIKING SEA)

OPERATIONS		SHIP		PERSONNEL	
Operator	Royal Cruise Line	Tons (grt)	28,000	Passengers	750
Flag	Bahamas	Length (ft)	676	Crew	410
Trade	World Wide	Beam (ft)	83	Nationality	
Built	1973	Draft (ft)	24	Officers	Greek
Renovated	1991	Knots	22	Crew	Greek

ACCESSIBILITY	OTHER	
SHIPBOARD: All decks accessible except uppermost Horizon (sports) Deck; ramped on inside of sill only with step down to outer deck. Public restrooms are not accessible.	Elevators 35'	4
	Able Comp Req'd?	YES
	Power Wheelchairs?	YES
HANDICAPPED CABINS: None	Tendering?	NO
	unless Captain OK's	

OTHER CABINS: Promenade Deck staterooms are best.
Cabin doors 23", 3" sills. Bathroom doors: 22"; 6" to 8" sills. Grabbars: tub & 17.5" high toilet.

ROYAL PRINCESS
(Good large ship in traditional "Love Boat" service and attentiveness.)

OPERATIONS		SHIP		PERSONNEL	
Operator	Princess Cruises	Tons (grt)	45,000	Passengers	1200
Flag	Brit.	Length (ft)	755	Crew	520
Trade	Panama/Europe	Beam (ft)	106	Nationality	
Built	1984	Draft (ft)	25	Officers	Brit.
Renovated		Knots	21	Crew	Int'l

ACCESSIBILITY	OTHER	
SHIPBOARD: Good accessibility (except launderette); 6 wheelchairs per cruise, public H/C bathrooms.	Elevators 35'	6
	Able Comp Req'd?	YES
HANDICAPPED CABINS: None per se, but cabin doors are 25" with low sills. Bathrooms have 21.5" doors and are 7" higher than cabin. AA Suites have 23.5" bathroom door.	Tendering?	NO
	unless Captain OK's	

ROYAL VIKING QUEEN
(Sistership of ulta deluxe Seabourn ships by the best of Royal Viking service.

OPERATIONS		SHIP		PERSONNEL	
Operator	Royal Viking	Tons (grt)	10,000	Passengers	212
Flag	Bahamas	Length (ft)	438	Crew	150
Trade	World Wide	Beam (ft)	62	Nationality	
Built	1992	Draft (ft)	16	Officers	Norway
Renovated		Knots	19	Crew	Eur.

ACCESSIBILITY	OTHER	
SHIPBOARD: No public H/C bath, but all else accessible.	Elevators (36")	4
	Able Comp Req'd?	YES
HANDICAPPED CABINS: (4) Beautiful 245 sq.ft. suites.	Tendering?	NO
Bergen Dk 5: #228 & 230, Stavenger Dk. 3, #332 & 334	unless OK'd by Capt.	
Ocean view from living & bedrooms, large picture windows.		

Twin beds convert to Queen-sized bed. Accessible bathroom has large vanity, handicapped toilet and shower. Ramped sill to bathroom, 35" doors. "Walk-in" closet is 20" wide.

ROYAL VIKING SUN
(Magnificent 5-star ship with freindly Scandinavian service)

OPERATIONS		SHIP		PERSONNEL	
Operator	Royal Viking	Tons (grt)	37,845	Passengers	758
Flag	Bahamas	Length (ft)	669	Crew	469
Trade	World Wide	Beam (ft)	95	Nationality	
Built	1988	Draft (ft)	23	Officers	Norway
Renovated		Knots	21	Crew	Eur.

ACCESSIBILITY	OTHER	

SHIPBOARD: Uppermost Deck not accessible, but others are including open deck areas aft and midship. Public restrooms are not accessible. Batteries for 3 wheel "Amigo" type power wheelchairs must be gel-celled (no wet cell or acid type).

Elevators (4)	36"
Able Comp Req'd?	YES
Power Wheelchairs?	YES
Tendering?	NO
unless OK'd by Capt.	

HANDICAPPED CABINS: (4)
Category F: #420, 422, 423, & 425
Four very spacious (264 sq. ft.) handicapped cabins with roll-in showers, and "wheel-in" closets. Entries to cabin and bathroom are 35" each with mattress height 19.5".

OTHER CABINS: Other stateroom entrances are 27 to 29" wide with 1" high sills; bathroom entries are 23: wide with 3 to 4" sills.

RYNDAM
(Sistership of STATENDAM; debuting in 1993, Trade TBD)

HANDICAPPED CABINS: (4) Spacious.

SAGAFJORD
(Ultra deluxe and comfortable, 5-star, low density classic ship.)

OPERATIONS		SHIP		PERSONNEL	
Operator	Cunard/NAC	Tons (grt)	25,147	Passengers	589
Flag	Bahamas	Length (ft)	620	Crew	352
Trade	World Wide	Beam (ft)	82	Nationality	
Built	1965	Draft (ft)	27	Officers	Norway
Renovated	1983	Knots	1920	Crew	Eur.

ACCESSIBILITY	OTHER	

SHIPBOARD: All decks accessible inside, but only the Lido on the Veranda Deck is accessible outside on the aft deck. A small outside area aft of the disco (Club Polaris) is also accessible.

Elevators: small 29"	4
Able Comp Req'd?	YES
Power Wheelchairs?	YES
(24" width limit)	
Tendering?	YES
(with Captain's OK)	

HANDICAPPED CABINS: (12)
Accessible to 22.5" and some 24" wheelchairs.
Low sills, but cabin doors are 26 to 27", and bathroom, 24 to 26". #121, 123, 218, 220, 225, 227, 235, 332, 334, 341, 343, & 363.

OTHER CABINS: Following cabins have no bathroom sill, but no turn room requires some mobility to access bathroom: #216, 201, 202, 267, 276, 278, 280, 353, 362, 364, 374, 381, 389, 433, 482, 484, 486, 488, & 490.

SAPPHIRE SEAS
(Short cruises provide less expensive sailings on classic style ship.
(EX; ATLANTIS, GEN'L W.P. RICHARDSON, LA GUARDIA, LEILANI, EMERALD SEAS)

OPERATIONS		SHIP		PERSONNEL	
Operator	Sea Fest Cruises	Tons (grt)	19,000	Passengers	920
Flag	Liberia	Length (ft)	623	Crew	400
Trade	Bahamas	Beam (ft)	75	Nationality	
Built	1944	Draft (ft)	26	Officers	N. Eur./Scand.
Renovated	1970 & 1991	Knots	15	Crew	Filipino

ACCESSIBILITY	OTHER	
SHIPBOARD: Some areas require some assistance over sills or coamings. No handicapped public restrooms.	Elevators	YES
	Able Comp Req'd?	YES
HANDICAPPED CABINS: (1)	Tendering?	NO
#S-20 with Shower (Category 2, Sun Deck)	unless Captain OK's	

SEABOURN PRIDE & SEABOURN SPIRIT
(Rated best cruise line by readers of Conde-Nast TRAVELER magazine.)

OPERATIONS		SHIP		PERSONNEL	
Operator	Seabourn Cruises	Tons (grt)	10,000	Passengers	204
Flag	Norway	Length (ft)	439	Crew	140
Trade	World Wide	Beam (ft)	63	Nationality	
Built	PRIDE in 1988	Draft (ft)	16	Officers	Norway
	& SPIRIT in 1989	Knots	18	Crew	Eur.

ACCESSIBILITY	OTHER	
SHIPBOARD: Well appointed luxury ship with good accessibility throughout. Public bathrooms are accessible.	Elevators 31"	3
	Able Comp Req'd?	YES
HANDICAPPED CABINS: (4) #134, 136, 232, &234	Power Wheelchairs?	YES
Very spacious (277 sq. ft.) suites are well appointed.	Tendering?	YES
Cabin entries are 31"; bathroom doors 27" with 3.5" sills.	with Captain OK	

SEABREEZE
(Inexpensive ship for short Bahama cruises.)(Ex: FEDERICO C, STARSHIP ROYALE)

OPERATIONS		SHIP		PERSONNEL	
Operator	Dolphin Cruise	Tons (grt)	15,483	Passengers	832
Flag	Panama	Length (ft)	607	Crew	350
Trade	Bahamas	Beam (ft)	79	Nationality	
Built	1958	Draft (ft)	28	Officers	Eur.
Renovated	1985	Knots	21	Crew	Int'l.

ACCESSIBILITY	OTHER	
SHIPBOARD: Most public rooms are accessible.	Elevators 29'	6
HANDICAPPED CABINS: None	Able Comp Req'd?	YES
	Tendering?	YES
OTHER CABINS: Bathrooms have 20" doors; cabins 22".	with Captain OK	

SEAWARD

(NCL's superb service and four large, very nice but inside only cabins
on modern, beautiful ship having large topside sun decks)

OPERATIONS		SHIP		PERSONNEL	
Operator	Norwegian Cr. L.	Tons (grt)	42,276	Passengers	1534
Flag	Bahamas	Length (ft)	700	Crew	630
Trade	Caribbean	Beam (ft)	96	Nationality	
Built	1988	Draft (ft)	23	Officers	Norway
Renovated		Knots	21	Crew	Int'l.

ACCESSIBILITY	OTHER	

SHIPBOARD: All decks accessible as are all the many activities, piano bars, lounges, arcades, etc. Public bathrooms are not accessible. Batteries for 3 wheel "Amigo" type power wheelchairs must be gel-celled (no wet cell or acid type).

Elevators 34-36"	3
Able Comp Req'd?	YES
Power Wheelchairs?	YES
Tendering?	NO
unless Captain OK's	

HANDICAPPED CABINS: (4)
Category #7: #4112, 4113, 4123, & 4124
Inside doubles with roll-in showers; cabin & bath doors are 36" wide. Sill heights are between 1.5" to 2".

SEAWIND CROWN

(Good refubishmentt of classic type ship provides an acre of open decks.)
EX: INFANTE DOM HENRIQUE, VASCO DA GAMA

OPERATIONS		SHIP		PERSONNEL	
Operator	Seawind	Tons (grt)	24,000	Passengers	624
Flag	Panama	Length (ft)	641	Crew	250
Trade	Caribbean	Beam (ft)	81	Nationality	
Built	1961	Draft (ft)	27	Officers	Eur.
Renovated	1988	Knots	17	Crew	Eur.

ACCESSIBILITY	OTHER	

SHIPBOARD: Excepting Uppermost Deck, all decks and activities are accessible.

HANDICAPPED CABINS: (2) #305 & 314
Handicapped cabins are outside doubles on OceanDeck with wide 34" doors.

Elevators 36'	4
Able Comp Req'd?	YES
Tendering?	NO
unless Captain OK's	

SENSATION

(See sistership FANTASY; planned debut 1993; Trade Caribbean)

HANDICAPPED CABINS: (20) Spacious on same deck.

SKY PRINCESS

(Large comfortable ship with good service in Princess tradition including good handicapped facilities.) (EX: FAIRSKY)

OPERATIONS		SHIP		PERSONNEL	
Operator	Princess	Tons (grt)	46,000	Passengers	1200
Flag	British	Length (ft)	789	Crew	563
Trade	Alaska/Caribbean	Beam (ft)	91	Nationality	
Built	1984	Draft (ft)	24	Officers	British
Renovated		Knots	22	Crew	Eur.

ACCESSIBILITY	OTHER	
SHIPBOARD: Assistance required in certain select areas and to outside decks.	Elevators 43"	6
	Able Comp Req'd?	YES
	Tendering?	YES
HANDICAPPED CABINS: (6) All outside doubles; 32" doors.	if Captain OK's	
Caribe Deck: #207 & 208		
Dolphin Deck: #136, 137, 160, & 161		

STAR PRINCESS

(Beautiful, large, modern ship wth superb Princess Cruise service has 10 spacious handicapped staterooms.)

OPERATIONS		SHIP		PERSONNEL	
Operator	Princess	Tons (grt)	63,524	Passengers	1470
Flag	Liberia	Length (ft)	806	Crew	600
Trade	Alaska/Caribbean	Beam (ft)	105	Nationality	
Built	1989	Draft (ft)	27	Officers	Italian
Renovated		Knots	22	Crew	Eur.

ACCESSIBILITY	OTHER	
SHIPBOARD: All decks are accessible including; Theatre, Beauty Salon, Gift Shops, Casino, Card room, library, Casino, etc.	Elevators 40"	9
	Able Comp Req'd?	YES
	Tendering?	YES
HANDICAPPED CABINS: (10) All very spacious, 32" doors Outside Doubles with roll-in showers. (236 to 244 sq. ft)	with Captain's OK usually rendered	
Dolphin Deck, Category D: #101, 102, 118, & 119		
Caribe Deck, Category D: #136 & 137		
Dolphin Deck, Category F: #138, 139, 140, & 141		

STAR/SHIP ATLANTIC

(Good value with short Bahama cruise package and Walt Disney World
tie-in with their Official Cruise Line for families.) (EX: ATLANTIC)

OPERATIONS		SHIP		PERSONNEL	
Operator	Premier Cruise	Tons (grt)	36,500	Passengers	1550
Flag	Liberia	Length (ft)	671	Crew	500
Trade	Bahama	Beam (ft)	90	Nationality	
Built	1982	Draft (ft)	25	Officers	Greek
Renovated	1988	Knots	24	Crew	Int'l.

ACCESSIBILITY	OTHER	
SHIPBOARD: Limited access to Sun Deck; elevators serve other decks from Bahamas to pool Deck. Boarding at Port Canaveral and Nassau are from special gangway on Restaurant Deck for wheelchair passengers.	Elevators 31"	4
	Able Comp Req'd?	YES
	Power Wheelchairs?	YES
	(dependent on type)	
HANDICAPPED CABINS: None	Tendering?	YES
OTHER CABINS: Cabin doors are 24"; but bathrooms have 6" sills.	(with collapsible chairs to Port Lucaya)	

STAR/SHIP MAJESTIC

(Good family value tie-ins with Walt Disney World; must use collapsible wheelchairs when
tendering to Port Lucaya.) (EX: SPIRIT OF LONDON, SUNPRINCESS)

OPERATIONS		SHIP		PERSONNEL	
Operator	Premier Cruise	Tons (grt)	17,750	Passengers	1006
Flag	Bahama	Length (ft)	536	Crew	370
Trade	Bahama	Beam (ft)	75	Nationality	
Built	1972	Draft (ft)	21	Officers	British
Renovated	1989	Knots	21	Crew	Int'l.

ACCESSIBILITY	OTHER	
SHIPBOARD: Limited access to Starlight Cabaret and Mercury Theatre. Aft elevator accomodates wheelchairs (35")' passageways are 37" wide. Wheelchairs may be use on Man-O-War, Green Turtle, Treasure, and Great Guana Cay; motorized carts for rent on Man-O-War Cay.	Elevators Aft one is OK.	
	Able Comp Req'd?	YES
	Power Wheelchairs?	YES
	(dependent on type)	
	Tendering?	YES
HANDICAPPED CABINS: None	(with collapsible chairs to Port Lucaya)	
OTHER CABINS: Bathrooms are inaccessible; cabin entry door is 24".		

STAR/SHIP OCEANIC

(Walt Disney World's Official Cruise Line with good family cruises.)

OPERATIONS		SHIP		PERSONNEL	
Operator	Premier Cruise	Tons (grt)	40,000	Passengers	1609
Flag	Bahama	Length (ft)	782	Crew	530
Trade	Bahama	Beam (ft)	96	Nationality	
Built	1965	Draft (ft)	28	Officers	Greek
Renovated	1993	Knots	26	Crew	Int'l.

ACCESSIBILITY	OTHER
SHIPBOARD: Premier-Main Deck, pool and bunge decks are accessible, but some other decks, including topmost deck are not. Dining Room entry only from aft.	Elevators: 23" fwd, 29" aft
	Able Comp Req'd? YES
	Power Wheelchairs? YES
	(dependent on type)
HANDICAPPED CABINS: (1)	Tendering? YES
Category 4, Restaurant Deck: #R-051 with roll-in shower.	(with collapsible chairs to
	Port Lucaya)
OTHER CABINS: Bathrooms have 3 to 6" sills, narrow doors. Following cabin entries are 28" with 1" sill: Premiere Dk: Cat. 7: P005, P006, P011, P012, P018, P019, Cat: 6: P003 & P004, Cat. 4: All Premier Deck ones. Continental Dk: C005, C006, C019, C023, C151, C154, C155, C156, C161, C162, & Corner C163 Restaurant Dk: Cat. 4: R050, R052, R053, R064, & R071 to R074. Atlantic Dk: A049, A054, A061, A068, A072, A075, A080, A085, A086, A088, A093, & A094	

STATENDAM

(First of Holland America's new class of ships with 6 excellent
handicapped staterooms each) (MAASDAM in 1993, RYNDAM in 1994)

OPERATIONS		SHIP		PERSONNEL	
Operator	Holland America	Tons (grt)	55,000	Passengers	1266
Flag	Bahama	Length (ft)	720	Crew	571
Trade	World/Caribbean	Beam (ft)	101	Nationality	
Built	1992	Draft (ft)	25	Officers	Dutch
Renovated		Knots	20	Crew	Indones/Filip

ACCESSIBILITY	OTHER
SHIPBOARD: Excellent facilities throughout for the handicapped on this beautiful new ship.	Elevators: All Accessible 8
	Able Comp Req'd? NO
	if self sufficient
	in emergency
HANDICAPPED CABINS: (6) Wide 36" doors, no sills. Lower Promenade Deck: C-389 & C-390 "A" Deck: G-704, G-706, G-709 & G -711; all with roll-in showers.	Power Wheelchairs? YES
	Tendering? YES
	if at all practicable

SUN PRINCESS

(Giant new Princess ship with handicapped cabins to have many dining choices, two main
show rooms, 3 pools, and more balconies than anyother ship afloat.)

OPERATIONS		SHIP		PERSONNEL	
Operator	Princess	Tons (grt)	77,000	Passengers	1950
Flag	TBD	Length (ft)	856	Crew	900
Trade	World/	Beam (ft)	106	Nationality	
Built	1995	Draft (ft)	26	Officers	Eur
Renovated		Knots	21	Crew	Int'l

TROPICALE
(Bright colors, younger cruisers favor this for fun & good value)

OPERATIONS		SHIP		PERSONNEL	
Operator	Carnival	Tons (grt)	36,674	Passengers	1396
Flag	Liberia	Length (ft)	669	Crew	500
Trade	Caribbean	Beam (ft)	86	Nationality	
Built	1981	Draft (ft)	23	Officers	Ital
Renovated		Knots	21	Crew	Int'l.

ACCESSIBILITY	OTHER	
SHIPBOARD: Public rooms have ramps and are accessible but assistance is requied overr steps to the Dining Room and over sills to open decks. Public toilets can not accommodate a wheelchair.	Elevators 36"	8
	Able Comp Req'd?	YES
	Power Wheelchairs?	YES
	Tendering?	NO
HANDICAPPED CABINS: None	unless Captain OK's	

OTHER CABINS: The following cabins have enlarged entryways to cabins and bathrooms but ramps are required over 6" sills to bath. Some ramps available; others can be made up. Bathrooms have grab bars and shower seats.
M66, M69, M116, U18, U21, U130, U133, E92, E93, E123

VIKING SERENADE
(Popular cruise ship with newly added accessible cabins provide affordable 3 & 4 night cruises.) (EX: SCANDINAVIA, STARDANCER)

OPERATIONS		SHIP		PERSONNEL	
Operator	Royal Caribbean	Tons (grt)	40,132	Passengers	1514
Flag	Bahama	Length (ft)	623	Crew	614
Trade	Baja Calif. (Mexico)	Beam (ft)	98	Nationality	
Built	1982	Draft (ft)	22	Officers	Eur.
Renovated	1991	Knots	20	Crew	Eur.

ACCESSIBILITY	OTHER	
SHIPBOARD: Excepting topside boat area on Club Deck and the Compass Deck (Viking Crown Lounge accessible by elevator), all other decks and activities are accessible with wide passageways (45") throughout.	Elevators	5
	wide doors; 34-49"	
	Able Comp Req'd?	YES
	Powered Chairs?	YES
HANDICAPPED CABINS: (4) Inside cabins (168 sq. f.) have 5' turn circle, 33" doors, no sills, roll-in showers, fold down seats.	Tendering?	YES
	With Captain OK's	
Category "M": #5037, 5547, & 5549. Category "P": 4035		

OTHER CABINS: No entry sill but still too narrow for all wheelchairs. Cabin door clearance is only 19"; bathroom 15" with 6 to 9" sill.

VISTAFJORD

(Classic 5-star Cunard/NAC ship with superb and friendly service.)

OPERATIONS		SHIP		PERSONNEL	
Operator	Cunard/NAC	Tons (grt)	24,492	Passengers	736
Flag	Bahama	Length (ft)	628	Crew	379
Trade	World Wide	Beam (ft)	82	Nationality	
Built	1973	Draft (ft)	27	Officers	Norway
Renovated	1983	Knots	20	Crew	Eur.

ACCESSIBILITY	OTHER
SHIPBOARD: All enclosed decks accessible but only Lido (Veranda) Deck is accessible without assistance.	Elevators: Small to 29" 6
	Able Comp Req'd? YES
HANDICAPPED CABINS: (44) For 22" and some 24" W/C	Power Wheelchairs? YES
Promenade Deck(B) #155, 156, 174, 176	(24" width limit)
Upper Deck (D) #205, 208, 243, 244;	Tendering? YES
(F) #201, 206, 274, 283, 285.	(with Captain's OK)
Main Deck: (G) #315, 317, 320, 341, 346, 348, 427, 428;	
(H) #440, 441; (I) 301, 302;	
(J) 316, 320; (K) 406, 426, 433, 434; (OC) 304, (PD) 435	
"A" Deck: (H) #503, 504, 518, 527, 542, 551, 568, 577;	
(K) 670; (L) 681, 690	
OTHER CABINS: Bathroom sills are 5" or higher	

WESTERDAM

(Gracious and friendly Holland America service.) (EX: HOMERIC))

OPERATIONS		SHIP		PERSONNEL	
Operator	Holland America	Tons (grt)	53,872	Passengers	1494
Flag	Bahama	Length (ft)	798	Crew	620
Trade	Carib./Alaska	Beam (ft)	83	Nationality	
Built	1986	Draft (ft)	21	Officers	Dutch
Renovated	1990	Knots	23	Crew	Indones/Filip

ACCESSIBILITY	OTHER
SHIPBOARD: All decks accessible but some parts of some decks require assistance. Some wheelchairs for rent at $3.50/day. Handicapped public restrooms.	Elevators: 31" 7
	Able Comp Req'd? NO
	if self sufficient.
HANDICAPPED CABINS: ((4) (Roll-in Showers)	Power Wheelchairs? YES
Large Staterooms: (Category D: #002 & 087; E: #068	Tendering? YES
Standard Size: (Category G: #021); all with roll-in showers	if Captain's OK's
OTHER CABINS: Upper Promenade cabins have 26" door entry (less that 1" sill) but bathroom door is 24" with 7" sill. Ramps are available on request as are portable commodes if desired.	

WINDWARD

(Lovely new ship with superb new handicapped facilities;
includes staterooms for the hearing impaired.)

OPERATIONS		SHIP		PERSONNEL	
Operator	Norwegian Cr.Line	Tons (grt)	41,000	Passengers	1246
Flag	Bahama	Length (ft)	623	Crew	480
Trade	Caribbean	Beam (ft)	94	Nationality	
Built	1993	Draft (ft)	22	Officers	Nor.
Renovated		Knots	21	Crew	Int'l

ACCESSIBILITY	OTHER	
SHIPBOARD: Excepting Sky Deck, all other decks and activities are accessible. No accessible public bathrooms. Batteries for 3 wheel "Amigo" type power wheelchairs must be gel-celled (no wet cell or acid type).	Elevators 34-36"	7
	Able Comp Req'd?	YES
	Power Wheelchairs?	YES
	Tendering?	NO
HANDICAPPED CABINS: (6)	unless Captain OK's	
There are no sills in handicapped cabins. Doors are 3' wide doors to cabin and roll-in shower bathroom in larger than standard cabins. There are special cabins for the hearing impaired.		
Norway Deck: #8041 & 8042 are 220 sq. ft. (Outside)		
Biscayne Deck: #5131 & 5132 are 198 sq. ft. (Inside)		
Atlantic Deck: #6107 & 6124 are 193 sq. ft. (Inside)		

ZENITH

(Beautiful new ship with grandly decorated public rooms.)

OPERATIONS		SHIP		PERSONNEL	
Operator	Celebrity	Tons (grt)	47,255	Passengers	1374
Flag	Liberia	Length (ft)	682	Crew	657
Trade	N. Amer	Beam (ft)	95	Nationality	
Built	1992	Draft (ft)	24	Officers	Greek
Renovated		Knots	21.4	Crew	Int'l

ACCESSIBILITY	OTHER	
SHIPBOARD: Sun Deck is not accessible, but others are.	Elevators (6)	YES
	Able Comp Req'd?	YES
HANDICAPPED CABINS: (4) large outside cabins well out-fitted for handicapped; 3' plus doors with negligible sills, roll-in shower. Europa Deck: #5048, 5049, 5060, 5061	Power Wheelchairs?	YES
	Tendering?	NO
	without Captain's OK	

PART III
RIVERS & CANAL BARGES

The smaller, ocean going cruise ships discussed in PART II, often cruise some of the deep, large rivers of the world: the Amazon and Orinoco in South America, the St. Lawrence in North America, a portion of the Yangste in China, the Thames in England. But with less draft, non-seagoing river boats cruise further up these same rivers as well as many other silt laden or shallower rivers that are inaccessible to the ocean vessels.

But accessible overnight river and canal barge vessels are seldom found. Much smaller on average than either ferries or ocean going cruise ships (1,300 vs. 6,700 and 17,000 tons, respectively), only a very small number of them have either handicapped cabins or even elevators and lifts between the two or three decks typically found on such vessels.

Table 23 lists river and canal barges with handicapped cabins aboard, both with and without elevators. Other boats without handicapped cabins but which have better-than-average accessibility are also listed there. They may have elevators or lifts between decks, or have some cabins located on the main dining and lounge deck. Table 24 lists the operators of these boats.

Depicted in Figure 10, the *Murray Princess*, a Mississippi River-type, old fashioned paddlewheeler cruises Australia's mightiest, and very scenic, Murray River. One of the world's most accessible river boats, a full ten percent of the 60 cabins aboard, complete with roll-in showers, are especially large and very well equipped for the handicapped. Elsewhere, the ship is well ramped with wide doors everywhere. There is an elevator between decks. The ship's colonial decor and the dress of their friendly crew . . . excepting their Australian accents . . . reflect America's

Table 23

River, Canal Barges, and sailing vessels with varying degrees of accessibility.

A. BOATS WITH HANDICAPPED CABINS OR BERTHS.

TYPE	PAX	SHIP'S NAME	LIFTS	CABINS	COUNTRY	TRADE
River	129	MURRAY PRINCESS	1	6	AUSTRALIA	Murray River
River	122	DRESDEN	0	1	GERMANY	Elbe River
Canal	8	DIONYSOS	1	1	FRANCE	Midi Canal
[1]Clipper	20	LUTGERDINA	1	7 berths	HOLLAND	Holland's waters
[1]Barque	16	STS LORD NELSON	1	8 berths	U.K./USA	Off shore, US & UK
River	420	AMERICAN QUEEN	2	Planned	USA	Mississippi

[1] Sailing vessels; see Part IV for more details.

B. BOATS WITH ELEVATORS OR PLATFORM/SEAT LIFTS BUT NO H/C CABINS.

TYPE	PAX	SHIP'S NAME	LIFTS	COUNTRY	TRADE
River	377	MISSISSIPPI QUEEN	2	USA	Mississippi
River	104	*SPIRIT of '98	1	ALASKA	Alaska Sightseeing
River	100	NORMANDIE	Platform	FRANCE	Seine
River	100	ARLENE	Platform	FRANCE	Saone/Rhone
River	128	CLARA SCHUMANN	Seat Lift	GERMANY	Elbe
River	128	THEODOR FONTANE	Seat Lift	GERMANY	Elbe
River	192	ITALIA	Seat Lift	GERMANY	Rhine

C. NO H/C CABINS NOR LIFTS BUT SOME CABINS ON DINING/LOUNGE DECKS.

TYPE	PAX	SHIP'S NAME	COUNTRY	TRADE
River	46	EXECUTIVE EXPLORER	USA	Columbia/Snake
River	60	CARIBBEAN PRINCE	USA	E. Coast/Carib.
River	64	NEW SHOREHAM II	USA	E. Coast/Carib.
River	66	CANADIAN EMPRESS	CANADA	St. Lawrence
River	88	SEA BIRD	USA/MEX	Baja/NW Rivers
River	90	SEA LION	USA/MEX	Baja/NW Rivers
River	112	HOLLAND	HOLLAND	Holland's waters
Canal	13	FLEUR de LYS	FRANCE	Rhone/Marne/Rhine
Canal	22	L'ABERCROMBIE	FRANCE	Saone
Canal	12	NAPOLEON	FRANCE	Rhone

D. CANAL BARGES WITH SPLIT LEVEL STEPS AND NO H/C CABINS.

TYPE	PAX	SHIP'S NAME	COUNTRY	TRADE
Canal	20	LITOTE	FRANCE	Burgundy Canal
Canal	12	HORIZON II	FRANCE	Burgundy Canal
Canal	12	TAURUS & SNIPE	ENGLAND	Various

* Former river boat *Victorian Empress* on St. Lawrence; now with Alaska Sightseeing as *Spirit of '98*. Cabins #108 and #112 have only 2" sill into small bathroom; others are 6".

Table 24
Operators/agents of accessible and other river and canal boats with limitations.

SHIP'S NAME	OPERATOR OR AGENT

A. BOATS WITH HANDICAPPED CABINS OR BERTHS.

MURRAY PRINCESS	Murray River Cruises, Captain Sturt Marine Goolwa, So. Australia 5214
DRESDEN	Dresdner Kreuzfahrten, Gmbh (0351) 441-5891 Dresden, Germany. FAX (0351) 441-5896
LUTGERDINA	Travel Agents International, 411 Carondelet St., New Orleans, LA 70130
DIONYSOS	Brock's Tours 80 Old Queens Anne Rd., Chattham, MA 02633
STS LORD NELSON	Jubilee Sailing Trust (See PART IV) N.O.A.H. 365 Thames St., Newport, RI 02840

B. RIVER BOATS WITH ELEVATORS OR PLATFORM/SEAT LIFTS.

SPIRIT of '98	Alaska Sightseeing, 2401 4th Ave., Ste. #700
(former *Victorian Empress*)	Seattle, WA 98121
MISSISSIPPI QUEEN	Delta Queen Steamboat Company #30 Robin St. Wharf, New Orleans, LA 70130-1890
NORMANDIE & ARLENE	Aqua Viva 30 Avenue Franklin-Roosevelt, 75008, Paris France

ITALIA,
  CLARA SCHUMANN &
  THEODOR FONTANE
	Rhine Cruise Agency
	Kohn-Dusseldorfer Deutsch Reheinschiffstadt AG
	500 Cologne, Germany

C. UPPER/MAIN BOARDING DECK CABINS WITH DINING ROOM & LOUNGE

CANADIAN EMPRESS	St. Lawrence Cruise Line, 253 Ontario St. Kingston, Ontario, Canada K7L 2Z4
EXECUTIVE EXPLORER	Yacht Ship Cruise Line, Inc. 520 Pike St., Suite 1610, Seattle, WA 98101
CARIBBEAN PRINCE & NEW SHOREHAM II	American Caribbean Cruise Line 461 Water St., Warren, RI 02885
SEA BIRD & SEA LION	Special Expeditions 133 E. 55th St., New York, NY 10022
HOLLAND	Sea Air Holidays, Ltd. Stamford, CT (800) 732-6247

FLEUR de LYS,
  L'ABERCROMBIE,
  NAPOLEON
	Abercrombie & Kent Int'l., Inc.
	1529 Kensington Road, Oak Brook, IL 60521-2141

D. CANAL BARGES WITH SPLIT LEVEL STEPS

LITOTE	Abercrombie & Kent Int'l. Inc. 1529 Kensington Road, Oak Brook, IL 60521-2141
HORIZON II	French Country Waterways, Ltd. P.O. Box 2195, Duxbury, MA 02331
TAURUS & SNIPE	Inland Waterway Holiday Cruises 56 Melbury Lane, Woodfield, Northampton, NN 4 RT, England

Figure 10
The MURRAY PRINCESS has 6 accessible Cabins

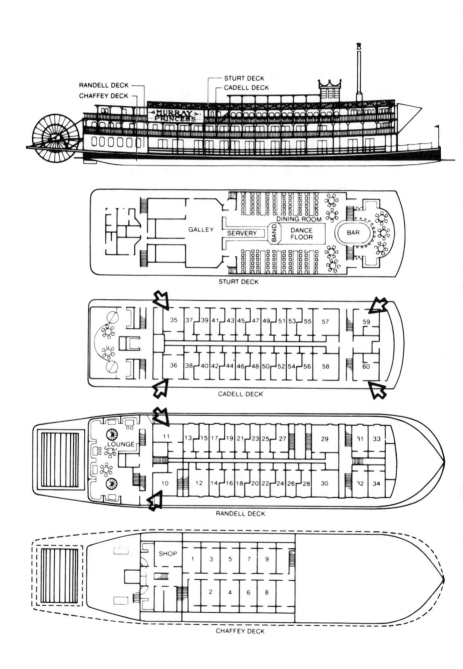

own lively and colorful past. Equally important, there is ramped access to all ports of call.

For the most part, European river boats have neither proper elevators nor handicapped cabins. The *Dresden* which normally cruises the Elbe from Dresden to Hamburg, does have a proper handicapped cabin on the same main deck as its main dining room and lounge. Other boats without handicapped cabins per se, do have railing-attached, fold-down seats or platform lifts between decks to aid those with partial mobility.

In France, the *Normandie's* platform provides access to the dining, stateroom, and topside sun decks on its history-steeped cruise on the Seine between Paris and the most delightful and picturesque artists' port city of Honfleur. Her sister, *Arlene,* cruises the Saone/Rhone rivers in the Provence, but her wheelchair platform does not reach to the sun deck.

In Germany, it's the Rhine and the old East Germany's newly opened Elbe river that are popular. KD's *Italia* has a railing-attached, fold-down seat for its Rhine cruises, but requires sliding over to that seat for transport between cabins, observation, and dining areas. It does not extend to the top sun deck, however. But those on the *Clara Schumann* and *Theodor Fontane* on the Elbe have seat lifts too, but their accommodations are a little better than the *Italia's*.

The paddlewheelers used in Australia, here at home, and elsewhere around the world, have an ancient and colorful history. Early ones were shown in a Roman bas relief in 600 A.D. and in China, a couple of hundred years later. But the biggest of them all (our own 4,500 ton-*Mississippi Queen* with towering funnels and many decks) has no wheelchair accessible cabins.

But help is coming. Delta Queen Steamboat Company now has the *American Queen* under construction. Much larger, this new paddlewheeler will also have several handicapped cabins when it is completed in 1995. The Mississippi, Missouri, and Ohio Rivers' 4,700 miles will soon be within easy cruising reach of all.

Further north, the much smaller paddlewheeler, *Canadian Empress* on the St. Lawrence, has one reasonably good cabin on the same deck as the dining, lounge, and observation areas, but does not have an elevator.

Some other river boats, with neither elevators nor handicapped cabins, do have a few Main Deck cabins adjacent to lounges and the dining rooms which offer interesting possibilities for the more able, physically adaptable, handicapped persons.

Canal barges are even less likely to be accessible. Smaller, and with fewer decks than their river boat cousins, only the *Dionysos* cruising in the shadow of the Pyrenees, has a large, well equipped handicapped cabin as well as a large elevator left over from its wine barrel carrying days.

South Australia's *Murray Princess* was mentioned earlier. In the pages ahead, other North American and European river boats and canal barges are described, beginning first with the American vessels cruising the inland waterways shown in Chart IX.

AMERICAN INLAND WATERWAYS

There are many historic and natural sights to see on many American waterways. Beginning with the St. Lawrence River, you can view the year-round herd of Beluga whales in Saguenay Fjord, (or catch the humpback whales in winter), and visit the historic sites of the "voyageurs" that settled and built the ramparts of old Quebec and Montreal.

Many of the ocean cruise ships listed in Part II take this voyage in the fall of the year, but turn back at Montreal. There are accessible day only excursions of from one to fifteen hours leaving from Montreal and Quebec City, but the *Canadian Empress* continues the journey, passing through the St. Lawrence Seaway's locks, past Boldt Castle, the Thousand Islands, and on into the Great Lakes.

It is a real joy to bed down in comfort and wake to the pleasant passing scene reminiscent of earlier days, and looking ahead to the new day. Unfortunately, the *Canadian Empress* has no elevator, nor proper handicapped cabins, but as shown in Figure 11, cabin #27 is the best and most convenient cabin located on the same boarding deck as the dining room, lounge, and observation areas. Rarely booked, it is held for physically handicapped with some mobility until the last minute.

Figure 11

The CANADIAN EMPRESS cruises the St. Lawrence.

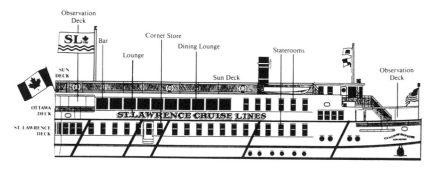

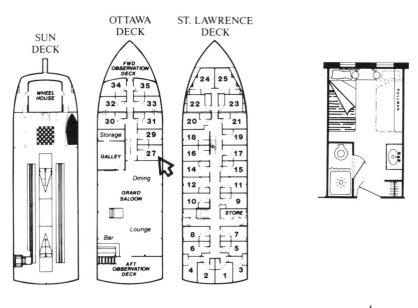

Chart IX
North American River and Canal Cruises.

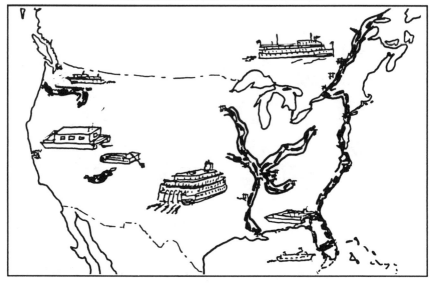

Mississippi and Other Heartland Rivers

She has elevators, is well ramped, and has some of the liveliest and best entertainment afloat, but the *Mississippi Queen*'s cabins are still only accessible for 22" wide wheelchairs. The cabins have a small step into the bathroom which has an even narrower 19" opening. The suites have bathtubs, but other cabins have small showers.

No interstate gambling, but like the nostalgic, old steam locomotives, she still makes quite a sight and sound. The steamboat whistle blows' round the bend from New Orleans to Minneapolis/St. Paul, up the Ohio to Pittsburgh, and on the Tennessee to the heart of the south.

Gambling elsewhere since Iowa started it in April of '91 with a fleet of 5 gambing boats (now down to 3), followed shortly with Illinois' large fleet of 9 vessels. In '93, Missouri too approved gaming on the river as did Indiana for 11 more including 5 on Lake Michigan, 5 on the Ohio, and one near French Lick; a bill is pending in Ohio . All of these gambling ships are accessible with elevators to all decks, but no overnight stays.

Louisiana limits gambling to only new vessels. Hilton's grand new entry in '94 will be the 2400 passenger casino ship *Queen of New Orleans*.

Delta Queen Steamboat Company's grand new 420 passenger *American Queen* will follow the same highly successful theme and cruise the same interstate waters as their *Mississippi Queen* (and the smaller *Delta Queen*)so there can be no gaming tables aboard. There will be a few elevators aboard and large accessible cabins for the handicapped with the exact number, not yet determined.

There are other day cruises on the Mississippi and its tributaries, but handicapped passengers are restricted to the main deck. The music trickles down the stairs, and an able companion, or other helping soul, can bring you something to slake your thirst. More important, the toilet facilities are usually on the Main Deck or on a ramped half deck away, but these are often not accessible.

An overnight journey of a different sort on the upper Mississippi from Davenport to Galena is on the *Julie Belle Swain*. The accommodations are ashore, however, with a handicapped hotel room and wheelchair-carrying bus for transport there and back.

Other American Rivers and Canals

Though small river boats have no elevators, some adventurous souls brave the few boats that have a few cabins on their main decks containing both dining room and lounge. The cabin doors are still usually only 22" wide with a sill to the small bathroom.

The same is true of the *Executive Explorer, Caribbean Prince*, and *New Shoreham II*, as well as the *Sea Bird* and *Sea Lion*. All five have large cabin windows and a forward observation lounge and dining room on the Main Deck as shown in Figure 12 for the *Executive Explorer*.

Using wheelchairs to go ashore at some stops is often a problem. The first three ships use bow ramps when beaching at small natural shores. The *Executive Explorer*'s ramp is larger than those of the other two, but is still only 25" at its narrowest point, with a step or two to get there.

Disembarking aft is not too much of a problem at some ports. The Jantzen Beach Red Lion docking in Portland, however, has two or three manageable steps (with an assist) to the ramp for the *Executive Explorer*. But it can be all but impossible in Alaska with its sometimes 25' tides that force boarding or disembarkation from one of the ship's upper decks.

Very stable in its beamy catamaran like hull, the *Executive Explorer* cruises the great Columbia and Snake Rivers of the Far West and also wanders up the coast to Alaska. The *Caribbean Prince* and *New Shoreham II* cruise more secluded areas of the Caribbean before wandering northward along the entire Eastern Seaboard, beginning in Miami and Florida's Keys, past the Everglades and southwest Florida's own ten thousand islands. They cross the state through many locks to Lake Okeechobee and on to the East coast to cruise up the Intracoastal Waterway to New York. They pass through the locks of the Erie Canal to enter Lake Ontario before entering other locks on the St. Lawrence on their way to the Saguenay River and Fjord again.

The *Sea Bird* and *Sea Lion* cruise the Columbia, Baja California, and other interesting coastal regions, often using rubber landing craft to reach more primitive shores.

As mentioned above for the *Executive Explorer*, some U.S. built river type boats depart to Alaska from Seattle, in contrast with the large number of foreign flagged cruise ships which must use Vancouver for their Alaska cruises. A new arrival on this scene is the *Spirit of '98* with Alaska Sightseeing. Not unlike the deck plans of the *Canadian Empress* shown earlier but larger and with a large (40" wide, 4' deep) elevator to serve three of its four decks, she has two cabins that have only 2" sills into their small bathrooms in lieu of the more commonly found 6" ones, (or the monstrous 9" one found in the Owner's Suite). The elevator, unfortunately, does not serve the topmost Sun Deck, but both port and starboard verandas are accessible from which to view the passing scene

Figure 12

EXECUTIVE EXPLORER has limited accessibility with Main Deck Cabins.

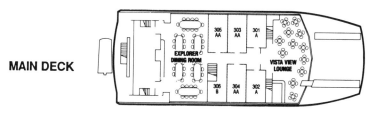

MAIN DECK

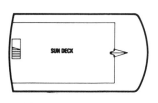

OBSERVATION DECK

BRIDGE DECK

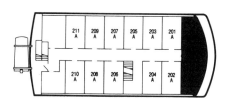

UPPER DECK

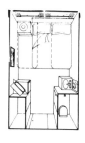

COLUMBIA & SNAKE
RIVER CRUISES;

Two large view
windows in cabins

RIVERS OF THE OLD WORLD

Except on one canal barge, there are no elevators, but there are some railing-attached platforms and seats for going between decks on the Old World's cruises depicted in Chart X.

Better than most with its railing-attached seat lift, the *Italia* shown in Figure 13, depicts a typical European river boat. With only 30' clearances under the bridges, most ship owners are loathe to add elevators for the three deck maximum that height allows. Typifying that attitude was the reply to my query about elevators on the largest of them all, the Volga River's five-deck *Akademik V. Glushkov*: "No problem; Russian sailors are strong." Volga boatmen!

The fold-down, provisioning platforms of the Seine's m/s *Normandie* and the Saone/Rhone River's m/s *Arlene,* readily handle wheelchairs between the dining, lounge, and stateroom decks. The *Normandie* also serves the topside sun and observation decks. There is ample room between cabin and lounge areas. The topside doors open electronically.

There is no sill on the 28" cabin doors, but the tiny bathroom's 24" width with three-inch sill and a five-inch step down along with a seven-inch shower sill, limits access only for those with limited mobility or an able assist using tips described later (i.e., stool transfers) in the small (9' by 13') cabins.

Turning eastward, you can also cruise the Rhine from Switzerland to the English Channel or the former East Germany's picturesque Elbe from Czechoslovakia to the North Sea. The Rhine's m/s *Italia* has a small, railing-attached, fold-down seat as do the newer one-meter draft *Clara Schumann* and *Theodor Fontane* on the shallow Elbe. They use pumpjets to protect the river bottom. When tied up, the earlier mentioned 91-passenger *Dresden* uses a ramped access to the handicapped cabin on the main dining deck; it has no elevators.

Other overnight, hotel-like river cruises on the Thames in England, the Shannon in Ireland, the Volga and Dneiper in Russia, or the Gota canal and river that cross Sweden, are not accessible to wheelchair users.

Chart X
History steeped European Rivers.

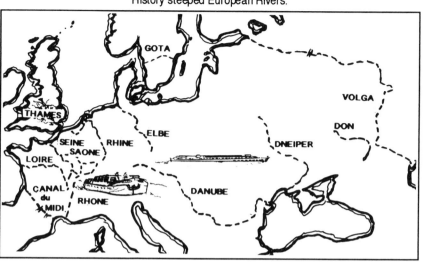

Figure 13
M/S ITALIA Seat Lift Provides Some Help.

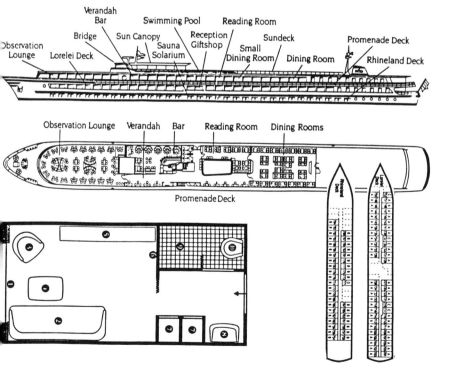

BARGE CANAL CRUISES

Deep canals linking the seas are regularly crossed by ocean-going cruise ships: the Panama Canal, Germany's Kiel Canal, Greece's Corinth Canal and, on round-the-world cruises, the Suez Canal. Many picturesque small canals are dotted with hotel barges and boats the French once called "Bateau mouche," or fly boats. The only fly in the ointment left is the shortage of good handicapped facilities.

One small canal barge with delightful, hotel-like service, however, does have a proper elevator and is completely wheelchair accessible. Larger than the other three staterooms, the one especially modified, handicapped stateroom in the *Dionysos* has a roll-in shower as shown in Figure 14. Vineyards, castles, and poppy fields are all there to enjoy as the *Dionysos* drifts by medieval towns on the 300 year old Midi Canal connecting the Mediterranean to the Atlantic near France's southwest border.

France's remarkable, and accessible, high speed train, the TGV, can whisk you there from Paris in just a couple of hours. It offers an en route taste of the latest and fastest in land travel, to contrast with one of the slowest and oldest. It is a most enjoyable means of hassle free travel near Spain's border. Today's unhurried gourmet diners may enjoy the best of French cuisine aboard, or stop in at the bistros along the way to taste the local wine or other tasty treats that made France a model of graceful living.

Most other hotel-type barges require the ability to negotiate a few narrow steps to the cabins located on a lower, inaccessible deck. But on some canal barges, a few cabins are located on the same upper deck as the dining room and lounge as shown in Figure 15, for example.

Two cabins on the upper deck of Abercrombie and Kent's *L'Abercrombie*, for example, and one each on their *Fleur de Lys* and the new *Napoleon,* provide access to the sun deck or an outer deck as well as to the main dining salon. The *L'Abercrombie* cruises the Saone in lower Burgundy of central France. The *Fleur de Lys* cruises the canals of Alsace

Figure 14
DIONYSOS; A Completely Accessible Canal Barge.

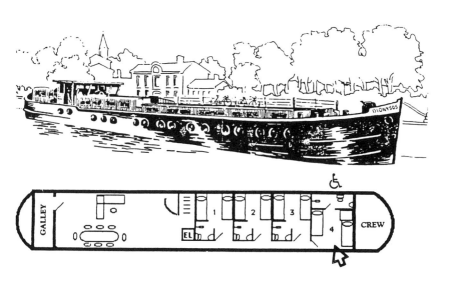

DIONYSOS

LENGTH:	95'
WIDTH:	17'
PASSENGERS:	8
CREW:	4

Figure 15
Canal Barges with upper, main deck cabins.

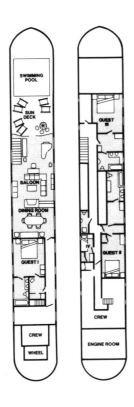

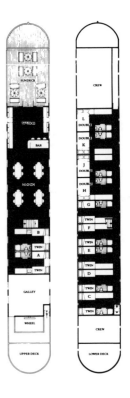

FLEUR DE LYS cruises the canals connecting the Rhine to the Rhône and Marne in Alsace.

L'ABERCROMBIE cruises t Saône in Burgundy.

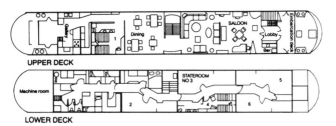

NAPOLEON cruises the Rhône in th Provence.

near Germany, while the *Napoleon* cruises the Rhone in the Provence of southern France.

Although most other canal barges have steep stairs, a few have split level decks. Those with the fewest stairs on split-level configurations are on Abercrombie and Kent's *Litote* and French Country Waterways' *Horizon II*. There are just four steps between cabin and lounge, but there are six from the lounge to *the Horizon II*'s sun deck. The cabin entrances have 26" wide doorways, the bathrooms, 24". The small shower door is only 21" wide. Both *Horizon II* and *Litote* cruise France's lower Burgundy region near Dijon.

Across the Channel in England, there are many, but far fewer accessible canal barges on its many rivers and canals. Rivers and connecting canals cut across the whole country from London to Bristol on the Irish Sea, Liverpool to the northwest and Leeds to the north, but the canals and locks handle only narrow canal boats.

An English canal boat's 7' width contrasts sharply with the Continent's 16' wide boats. They have very large windows, but there is no room for the wheelchair in the tiny train-sized quarters, and no room for en suite facilities. Showers and toilets are shared in the following, tandem towed "butty."

The *Taurus* and *Snipe* operated by Inland Waterway Holiday Cruises, for example, are one such pair of boats. The crew is most helpful however, as the English are wont to be, and eager to help with the few stairs at all the lunch and evening stops. Others stretch their legs alongside, but you can roll your wheels to one of the nearby shops or local pubs for a taste of the country and its most pleasant people if . . . you can handle the inaccessible facilities.

For-hire or bare-boat charters ("sans permis" in France) discussed in Part IV (e.g., the *Louisane* on France's Maine/Anjoy rivers) are more accessible than others, and are great in every other way.

PART IV
SMALLER BOATS

On the smallest of sailboats, you fold up the wheelchair and slide or bump around. Power-driven boats are not much better except on party, pontoon or houseboats. There you can wheel right aboard and be quite at home, never leaving your own chair.

There are larger sailing vessels equipped to handle wheelchairs. Elevators, and bunks or berths for the handicapped along with the small crew make for real sailing adventure and hands-on control. There's no need to be an A.B. (able-bodied seaman); the quietness and romance of the playing wind and sea are all there to enjoy close-in with as much fun as the most joyous of old salts.

Sailing

Steady as she goes, but sailboats are not on the level. The sails dramatically steady the boat's motion in any kind of sea. But you need a comfortable seat to buck the steady list. With muscled legs, it is easy enough to lock your knees and brace yourself against the leeward side, but impossible to do without legs or motor neurons. So you slide around to the lower leeward side, inches from the water, and hope that the rail is not awash, nor the spray too cold.

Necessity . . . the mother of invention. Founded in 1986, the National Ocean Access Project (NOAP, Annapolis City Marina, Suite 306, 410 Severn Ave., Annapolis MD 21403) has conceived innovative ways to aid the handicapped sailor. One design uses a molded fiberglass seat that doesn't require shifting sides on every tack. When comfortably strapped into a balanced, partially reclining seat, (including a place for your legs), the whole seat swivels around a vertical mounting post for each new tack to keep you on the high windward side. Handicapped sailors now keep the helm and compete here and abroad on equal footings.

Apart from fun sailing, competitions add excitement to the sport. The International Foundation for Disabled Sailing (with International Trophy Races) held a regatta during the Para-Olympic Games in Barcelona in '92. In '93, the World Championships will be held in Boston. The United States Yacht Racing Union has also established an **Independence Cup** regatta held annually for sailors with disabilities.

NOAP's nine chapters listed in Table 25 include locations from Canada and Alaska south to Texas, and from Boston in the east to California out west.

Equally exciting are the two larger sailing vessels listed earlier in Part III. On the *Lord Nelson,* a permanent crew of seven (including a Registered Nurse or doctor) can accommodate up to eight others in wheelchairs, who pitch in to handle many of the chores of sailing this large (141 ft.) British-built, three-masted, 400-ton barque operated by the Jubilee Sailing Trust Inc.

With sufficient interest, the non-profit American Friends of the Jubilee Sailing Trust join together with NOAP to charter the boat for sailing in the warmer American waters. The boat has flat decks, no steps, and hydraulic lifts between decks. There are two special lavatories and showers below, a library, and wide enough passages for wheelchairs both above and below the decks. You can even "climb the rigging like your daddy used to do" up the foremast in a special seat if you wish. (Operation N.O.A.H., 365 Thames St., Newport, RI 02840).

Across the ocean in Holland, the 110' *Lutgerdina* is an 1897 clipper re-outfitted as a teaching sailboat with accommodations for 7 wheelchair persons along with 13 other passengers. Sailing in the Zuider Zee, visiting picturesque Markham et al, the permanent crew of 3 demonstrates and teaches the handling of sail boats for 2 weeks with stopovers at Robinson Crusoe Island. There, the Holland Aquatic Sports Foundation teaches handling of canoes, kayaks, sail, and power boats. Individuals are then free to move on to sailing their own small boats in their own home waters.

Table 25
NOAP's self-help sailing clubs

NATIONAL OCEAN ACCESS PROJECT (NOAP)

PRESIDENT	Steve Spinetto		
INFORMATION	Ed Harisson		
	P.O. Box 33141, Farragut Station, Washington, DC		
CHAPTERS			
New Brunswick, CAN	Operation Able/Sail	Michael Dunn	(506) 857-3988
Anchorage, AL	Challenge Alaska	Patrick Reinhard	(907) 563-2658
Morro Bay, CA	Morro Bay Yacht Club	Gordon Carns	(805) 772-3981
Chicago, IL	Chicago Chapter	Ted Sullivan	(312) 294-2270
Houston, TX	Houston Area Chapter	Vince Morvillo	(713) 334-1993
Boston, MA	Courageous Sailing Center	Dru Slattery	(617) 725-3263
Boston, MA	Community Boating, Inc.	Barbara Rose	(617) 523-1038
New York, NY	Sea Legs	Ken Craig	(718) 987-6837
Annapolis, MD	Chesapeake Accessible Boating	Mike Garfinkel	(410) 974-2628

Houseboats and Pontoon (Party) Boats

The Micronesians and Polynesians had the right idea: simple, yet elegant. Use a second hull to obtain sea-worthiness, stability, and speed. No large beamy hulls for roll stability. Adapted to a powered boat, the use of two hulls is an ideal platform for the wheelchair person.

The broad, flat deck atop two pontoons is a stable houseboat, party, or pontoon boat. It is great in bays and rivers. Better yet is the ease of boarding by just wheeling the wheelchair through a side opening onto the broad, open, uncluttered deck.

If in dry storage, and before the crane or fork-lift operator lowers the boat into the ever changing water level, have him stop the boat at the same level as the pier. You can then roll right onto the level deck. Once aboard, there are no coamings, sills, narrow doors, or impediments to your freedom and no need to transfer to another seat. For Nature's call, there is a curtained screen for privacy around the built-in or portable toilet.

Rafting and Canoeing

Some other activities for the physically handicapped are a splash closer to the water. NOAP on the East Coast, and some western travel agencies listed later in Part V, specialize in handicapped tours that include canoeing, rafting, and other water activities for the disabled.

Bathroom accessibility, however, can be a problem. In certain regions of the country, hot and dry weather dehydrates everyone, so it's usually no problem there. If you "must," you can always go for a "swim" in the chilly water; there is a lot of water in the rivers. On some rivers, there are handicapped restrooms and stops along the way.

PART V
CRUISE TIPS

From John Masefield's *Sea Fever:* "I must go down to the seas again, to the lonely sea and the sky . . . " It is the call of the Sirens, the sea, a foreign shore. Lorelei's call.

But what to wear, where on board, large ship or small, where to, and who's who on board? With different emphasis, the popular guides on ocean cruising from Berlitz, Frommer and Fodor all cover these subjects well.[1][2][3]

But what about river boats, canal barges and long distance, overnight ferry trips? There is not much in these guides about such voyages. Some guides have a few pages on river boats and barge canal cruises, but there is very little or no coverage of the long-distance "cruise/ferries."

Nor is there much specific help and information directly affecting a handicapped person's ability to travel. All these guides contain a few token pages, but more is needed.

The last major part of our guide, therefore, includes some more general source references, and a description of the important pre-, post- and on-board shipboard activities from the perspective of a handicapped traveler.

[1] Berlitz Complete Guide to CRUISING AND CRUISE SHIPS, Douglas Ward, Berlitz Publishing Company, NY, NY.

[2] CRUISES AND PORTS OF CALL, Daniel and Sally Grotta, Fodor's Travel Publications, Inc., NY, NY.

[3] FROMMER'S CRUISES '91-'92, Marilyn Springer & Donald Schulz, Prentice Hall Press, NY, NY.

THE HANDICAPPED'S PROBLEMS

A handicapped person's problems are real, but they all differ. Some can stand and walk a few feet, others cannot. Thus, for a person on crutches or who is weak in his knees but can stand, high beds, toilet seats with wide-straddled grab bars, and grossly extended, "handicapped" sinks, all ease their plight. But for those others without gorilla-sized arms, extra padding in their chairs, or who don't like their shorter legs dangling, these so-called aids are less "convenient" than standard toilets and sinks, **IF** they can get adjacent to them. Thus only the individuals with a handicap know their unique situations and abilities to adapt to them. They've lived with whatever disability they have, tested it, and worked out ways to work around many problems. No standard is therefore espoused here for what is best or most accessible for any one individual.

Wheelchair widths and heights vary. Disabled community spokespersons press hard for roll-in showers. With no control of your legs, try to sit on a stool, hang on with one hand, and shower with the other. Many paraplegics, including the co-author and even a former President, prefer the comfort and security of a bathtub. (The only two bath tubs in the US Navy were installed for Franklin D. Roosevelt on the *USS Iowa (BB41)* and *USS Quincy (CA75)* in WWII for the Casablanca and Yalta conferences respectively). Bathtubs (with "bathboards" for those wanting to shower) offer the best of both worlds. They eliminate the need for shower sills too! But the often elevated (with plumbing underneath) and sometimes deeper than regular sea-going bathtubs are more difficult to handle.

The biggest problems all the physically handicapped face however, is the simple inability to get somewhere. This guide therefore, emphasizes the fundamental problem of steps or stairs, narrow door widths, and high coamings or sills used to control potentially free-standing water.

High coamings are found at watertight bulkheads and to all topside deck openings. Well protected openings to the main pool deck areas are often ramped. Elsewhere, staff members are always near, quick to assist.

Of all the barriers aboard ship, the most restrictive ones are in the small private staterooms and their particularly small bathrooms. A brief later section describes these handicapped cabins and their baths in more detail.

ADA recommends five-foot-diameter turning circles in baths and rooms. Some ships meet this grand recommendation, but practically speaking, that is more generous than found in most of the homes of the handicapped persons themselves. Like more costly circular driveways, they are nice to have, but if you can enter a bath or cabin, you can exit them.

Only the more basic door-width opening, steps and unramped sill heights were therefore considered throughout this guide as presenting serious barriers to paraplegics unable to walk.

Additional information is available from the ferry or cruise lines themselves on which passage is booked. The data obtained from the various line agents however, are often in error (e.g., some fail to allow for the door jambs and interference of the door itself, but the latter can be removed and stowed by the engineering staff).

As remarked earlier, Mr. Tom Gilbert and especially Mr. Kevin Anthoney more recently have given considerably more attention to detailed access measurements aboard cruise ships. Both gentlemen have published data but continue their services as private consultants. [1] [2]

Costs, and some Savings for the Handicpped

Cruise ship fares vary from $100/day/person to upwards of $1000/day for penthouses on the super luxury ships. For ferries, it is typically $10/hour of crossing time for a car and $5/hour for each passenger. In Florida, the $6.50 per day parking fee is waived for the handicapped.

Apart from providing larger staterooms for the handicapped, or letting them travel in a higher category cabin for the same fare, there are other savings for the handicapped.

Ferry lines often offer a 10% discount for the handicapped. In Europe and some St. Lawrence River ferries, other lines allow the accompanying attendant or companion to travel gratis (2 for 1). On some European Channel crossings, the handicapped person's hand-controlled car, or van with lift is transported free of charge.

[1] Kevin M. Anthoney, Cruise Consultants Int'l, 1527 Yale St.,Ste #3
   Santa Monica, CA 90404-3624
[2] Tom Gilbert, Consultant for the Disabled, P.O. Box 15648,
   Tampa, FL 33684-5648

HANDICAPPED RELATED ORGANIZATIONS

Travel Agencies

Twin Peaks Press has a more extensive list of the travel agencies that have worked with the handicapped; those listed below are especially noteworthy with some arranging such tours for two or three decades (Flying Wheels Travel & Evergreen Travel). Other listed organizations provide escort service, and others arrange for dialysis and oxygen on special cruises.

Table 26

Goup tour, Travel Agents, or activity organizers specializing in Handicapped Travel

(1)(2)**ACCESSIBLE JOURNEYS**
Howard McCoy, 35 W. Sellers Ave.
Ridley Park, PA 19078, (215) 521-0339

ALTERNATE MOBILITY ADVENTURE SEEKERS (AMAS)- (rafting, canoeing)
Boise State Univ.-PE Dept,
1910 University Ave.
Boise, ID 83725, (208) 385-3030

ANGLO CALIFORNIA
Helen Jones & Betty Schmidt
4250 Williams Rd., San Jose, CA 95129
(408) 257-2257

ASSOCIATED TRAVEL SERVICE
3465 W. Mill Rd., P.O. Box 09027
Milwaukee, WI 53209
(414) 351-1015, (800) 535-2045

DIRECTIONS UNLIMITED
Lois Bonnani
720 N. Bedford Rd., Bedford Hills, NY 10507
(914) 241-1700, (800) 533-5343

EVERGREEN TRAVEL
Jack & Betty Hoffman
4114-198 St., SW, Lynnwood, WA 98036
(206) 776-1184, (800) 435-2288

FLYING WHEELS TRAVEL
Edna Cook/Barbara Jacobson, PO Box 382,
Owatona, MN 55060, (800) 535-6790

HINSDALE TRAVEL SERVICE
Janice Perkins, 201 E. Ogden Ave. #100
Hinsdale, IL 60521 (708) 469-7349

C.W.HOGG (rafting, canoeing)
Idaho State Univ. Box 8118
Pocatello, ID 83209, (208) 236-3912

JUMPING MOUSE CAMP (rafting)
Ann Wheat, 1946 W. Morningside Drive
Phoenix, AZ 85023 (602) 262-2543

(2)**MEDICAL ESCORT INTERNATIONAL**
P.O. Box 8766
Allentown, PA 18105 (800) 255-7182

(1)**NAUTILUS TOURS**
Yvonne & Lou Nau, 5435 Donna Ave.,
Tarzana, CA 91356 (818) 343-6339

S'PLORE (rafting, canoeing)
Angela Mueggler
699 E. South Temple, Ste. 120
Salt Lake City, UT 84102 (801) 363-7130

TAILORED TOURS
Julia Brown
P.O. Box 797687, Dallas, TX 75379
(800) 628-8542, (214) 612-1168

THE CRUISE COMPANY
33 Lewis St., Greenwich, CT 06830
(203) 622-0203   (800) 825-0826

(2)**TRAVELING NURSES NETWORK**
P.O. Box 129, Vancouver, WA 98666
(206) 694-2462

(1) Publishes newsletters too.
(2) Nurse and escort service.

Other special: Dialysis at Sea (800) 544-7604 and Life Unlimited (305) 566-3991 for oxygen.

Newsletters and other handicapped related organizations.

All the organizations and newsletters listed below are a source of helpful information to the handicapped. Travelin'Talk, a self-help network of members throughout the country and abroad, provides other useful information for the handicapped too, and now solicits travel experiences from its members. Absorbing the former *Itinerary Magazine, Mainstream* is expanding their handicapped product and service information to include more travel news. *Access, Travel Health & Disability Institute* and *Twin Peaks Press* publish and distribute books and pamphlets useful to the handicapped. *SeaSpray Publishing* (cruises, but not necessarily handicapped) and *The Very Special Traveler* (all types of handicapped travel) newsletters describe first-hand travel experiences very candidly.

Table 27
Newsletters and other handicapped related organizations of interest.

*ACCESS (H/C Pubs & Info)
(Foundation .. Accessibility by .. Disabled)
P.O. Box 356, Malverne, NY 11565
(516) 887-5798, (800) 876-2882

HANDICAPPED TRAVEL NEWSLETTER
P.O. Box 269, Athens, TX 75751

MAINSTREAM
P.O. Box 3705598, San Diego, CA 92102

*MOBILITY INTERNATIONAL, USA
P.O. Box 3551 (Int'n'l Study Program)
Eugene, OR 97403 (503) 343-1284

MOSS REHABILITATION HOSPITAL
1200 W. Tabor Road
Philadelphia, PA 19141 (215) 456-9600

NATIONAL HANDICAPPED SPORTS
5201 N. 19th Ave.,Phoenix, AZ 85014
747 Third Avenue,New York, NY 10017

PARALYZED VETS OF AMERICA
PVA/ATTS Program 801 18th St,NW
Washington, DC 20006
(202) 416-7708, (800) 424-8200

PARAPLEGIC NEWS
5201 N, 19th Ave., Phoenix, AZ 85015
747 Third Ave., New York, NY 10017

REHABILITATION INT'R'N'T''L, USA
20 West 40th Street
New York, NY 1001

SEA SPRAY PUBLISHING COMPANY
RD 2 Box 736,
Sussex, NJ 07461

*SATH (Society for Advancement Travel for the Handicapped)
347 Fifth Ave, Suite 610
New York, NY 10016 (212) 447-7284

THE VERY SPECIAL TRAVELER
Box 166, 90 W. Montgomery Ave.
Rockville, MD 20850

*TIDE'S IN (Travel Industry and Disabled Exchange)
5435 Donna Ave., Tarzana, CA 91356

TRAVEL HEALTH & DISABILITY INST.
1269 El Camino Real, Suite 254
Menlo Park, CA 94026
(415) 321-9110

TRAVELIN' TALK (co-op network)
P.O. Box 353, Clarksville, TN 37043.
(615) 358-2503

TWIN PEAKS PRESS (Handicapped pubs)
P.O. Box 129, Vancouver, WA 98666
(206) 694-2462, orders only-(800) 637-2256

* Also conducts special tours.

The Destinations

If planning your own trip, the tourist or travel bureaus of various cities, states, provinces, and countries all provide a wealth of information on accommodations, sights, and transportation. Tourist bureaus and other related handicapped organizations are listed in Table 28. A more extensive list of such organization which includes access guides throughout the US and in many other cities and countries throughout the world is availble from Rehabilitation International, U.S.A.[1].

The cruise guide books cited earlier also provide excellent reference material for many cruises and their destinations. There is a choice of several cruise lines, ships large or small, and in many instances, river boats and ferries too.

For an Alaskan cruise for example, you can select from any of the 20 or so cruise ships operating there in late spring and the summer. The *Crown Princess,* one of the largest afloat, cruises there then. Or you can board one of the smaller all suite luxury ships, or even a river type boat to visit even smaller villages en route along the Inland Passage. You can reach even further into the remotest regions not visited by any other passenger ship in an expeditionary type ship (*Frontier Spirit*).

Alternatively, you may drive on an accessible ferry from Seattle to Victoria Island, then island hop up to Prince Rupert on BC Ferries before switching to one of Alaskan Marine Highway's ferries on your continuing Alaskan drive/float tour, choosing to sleep in accessible cabins either aboard or ashore. But book early, these car ferry trips are popular.

Holland America and Princess Cruises (the "Love Boat" line) together operate half the ships at that time of year, each with a variety of choices and all with good handicapped facilities. The only choices at other times of the year are the accessible ferries described earlier in Part I.

[1]Rehabilitation International, USA, 20 West 40th St. New York, NY 10018

Table 28
Handicapped and Tourist Bureaus of popular destinations.

ALASKA
Challenge Alaska
P.O. Box 110065, Anchorage
AK 99511-0065 Tel: (907) 563-2658

AUSTRALIA
Australian Tourist Commission
2121 Ave. of the Stars, Ste 450
Los Angeles, CA 90067, (310) 552-9566
**Australian Council for Rehab.for Disabled
NSW Div, PO Box 185, Epping, NSW 2121**

CANADA
Canadian Government of Tourism
1251 Ave. of the Americas, NY, NY 10020

(212) 757-3558

**Access Tourisme – Quebec
Keroul, P.O. Box 1000, Station M
Montreal, QC HIV 3R2 (514) 252-3104**

**Can.Rehab Comm.for Disabled & Elderly
45 Sheppard Ave. E, Ste. 801
Toronto, Ont., M2N 5W9(415) 250-7490**

DENMARK
Danish Tourist Bureau, 655 Third Ave.
New York, NY 10017, (212) 949-2333
**Society & Home for Disabled
Borgervaenget 7, DK-2100, Copenhagen**

FINLAND
Finnish Tourist Board, 655 Third Ave.
New York, NY 10017, (212) 949-2333
**RI Finnish Comm.InsuranceRehab. Agen.
Asemaihenkatu 3, 00520 Helsinki 52**

FRANCE
French Government Tourist Office
610 Fifth Ave., New York, NY 10020-2452
(212) 757-1125

**Comite Nationale Francais de Liaison
Readaptee Handicapes
38 Boulevard Raspail, 75007, Paris**

GERMANY
747 Third Ave., New York, NY 10017
(212) 308-3300

**Bundesarbeitsgemeinschaft Hilfe fur
Behinderte e.v.
Kirschfeldstrasse149, D-4000 Dusseldorf**

GREAT BRITAIN
British Tourist Authority
40 W. 57th St., New York, NY 10028
(212) 581-4700

**Royal Assoc. Disability & Rehabilitation
25 Mortimer Street, London, W1N 8 AB**

IRELAND
Irish Tourist Board, 757 Third Ave.
New York, NY 10017, (212) 418-0800

**Irish Wheelchair Association
Blackheath Dr., Clontarf, Dublin 3**

ITALY
Italian Government Travel Office
630 Fifth Ave., New York, NY 10011
(212) 245-4822

**Italian Assoc. for Assistanceto Spastics
Via Cipro 4/H, 00136 Rome**

NETHERLANDS
Netherlands Board of Tourism
355 Lexington Ave., New York, NY 10017
(212) 370-7367

**National Tourist Office
Central Documentation Dept.
Bezuidenhoutweg 2,2594AV, TheHague**

NORWAY
National Tourist Office, 655 Third Ave.
New York, NY 10017, (212) 949-2333
**Norges Handikapforbund
Nils Hansens Vei 2, Oslo 6**

SPAIN
Spanish National Tourist Office
Ste. 1850, 1221 Brickell Ave.
Miami, FL 33131

**National Institute of Social Services
Maria de Guzman 52, Madrid 3**

SWEDEN
Swedish National Tourist Office
655 Third Ave., New York, NY 10017
(212) 949-2333

**Swedish Central Committee for Rehab.
Box 303, S-161 26 Bromma**

THE SHIP'S CREW AND STAFF

Most crew members are part of the hotel staff; only one fourth to one third of the crew actually operate the ship. The Captain has overall responsibility while giving particular attention to the operation and safety of the ship itself. As depicted in Figure 16, aiding him directly on the Bridge are the Navigators and Chief Radio Officer. The Chief Engineer and his crew are responsible for the mechanical care and operation of all of the ships propulsion, utilities, and safety and integrity of the hull itself.

The care and attention to the passengers are the responsibility of the Hotel Manager and his large staff of pursers and stewards. Many of that staff are not cruise line employees but sign on as contract labor to firms specializing in that business. Hotel staff employees sign on for from four to nine month tours followed by several months leave (The widely used Filipino crew members usually are locked into a year of service).

The Tour Director is also not generally directly affiliated with the line, but is an independent contractor as are often the Ship's Photographer and other concessionaires. The Cruise Director plans all shipboard activities.

Some cruise lines add a gracious touch by having charming Hosts spend their time with more mature or elderly ladies not traveling in the company of a man. Often widowers, they must be good converstionalists and dancers, and, never be caught in the company of a younger lady passenger.

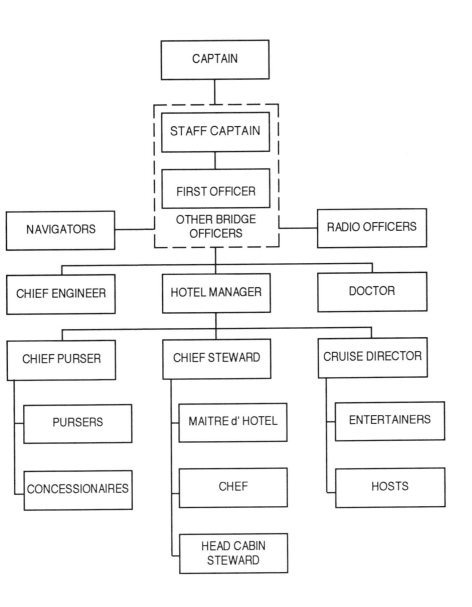

Figure 16
Ship's and Hotel's Staff and Crew.

THE ACCOMMODATIONS

Once described by Charles Dickens as a "preposterous box," staterooms are larger now, but still average only 125 sq.ft. per cabin including "en suite" facilities. Handicapped staterooms however, are much larger on all ships.

Figure 17 for example, depicts the layout of an excellent handicapped stateroom on RCCL's popularly priced *Monarch and Majesty of the Seas.* Full five foot turning circles are provided in both cabin and bath as well as other considerations for the handicapped.

Figure 17
Monarch of the Seas New Handicapped Stateroom

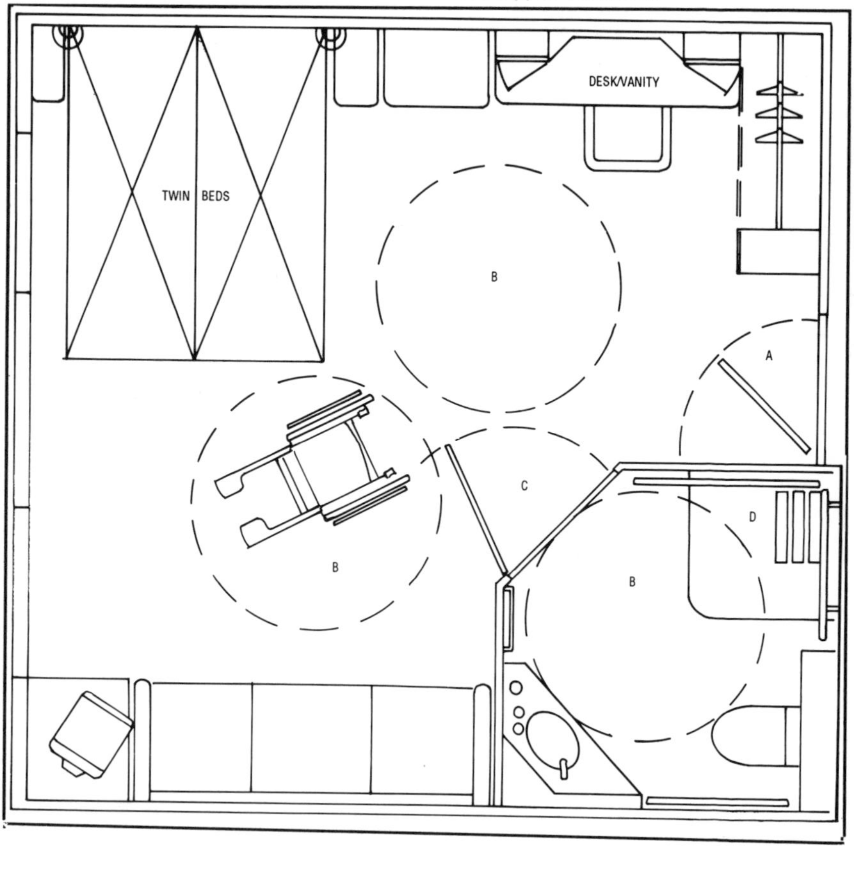

Exemplifying some of the best accommodations on first-class ships are those on Royal Viking's world-circling, 5-star *Royal Viking Sun* shown in Figure 18. With comfortable sitting room and a total area of 264 sq.ft., the suite is more than double the industry's standard cabin size. The cabin, closets, and bathroom are "roll-in" with 35" wide door entrances.

Figure 18
Royal Viking Sun's wheelchair accessible stateroom.

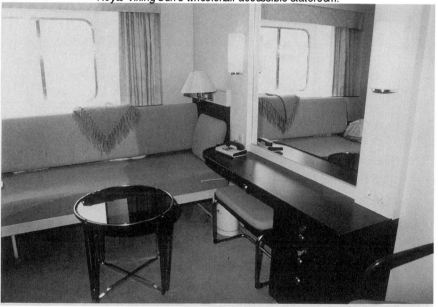

Luxury suites on some of the latest luxury ships have verandas, private sitting rooms, in-cabin safes, mini-bar with refrigerator, etc. But far smaller are the accommodations on ferries. The most luxurious suites on super ferries rival the most luxurious on cruise ships with deck-to-ceiling windows, private spas, and saunas.

The average ferry cabin, however, provides minimal accomodations. Figures 19 illustrates the four-person, bunk-type cabin on Prince of Fundy's *Scotia Prince* that is used as a double for handicapped persons. A portable ramp is used over the 7' high sill to the 6' x 7' bathroom with roll-in shower. The bathroom door opens into the cabin which though small, is larger than the average-sized double. Very little locker or closet space is provided, but ferry journeys are short.

Figure 19
Handicapped accommodations on the Bay of Fundy's Scotia Prince.

The Bathroom

The roll-in shower bathroom for Norwegian Cruise Line's *Seaward,* shown in Figure 20 below, depicts well the type of handicapped facilities found aboard some ships. Fold-down seats are used in the roll-in showers; there is a sloping deck or small sill for drainage. With bathtubs, small stools, or "bathboards" straddling the tub may be used for showering.

Figure 20
Roll-in showers and folding assistance bars on Norwegian Cruise Line's *Seaward*

LIFE ABOARD

At the Port of Embarkation

Prior to departure, a cruise information packet is mailed which contains all of the information needed for connecting flights (if on an Air/Sea package), and the location of the port of embarkation for those driving where valet parking and free parking is available for the handicapped.

Passengers or porters take the tagged bags just inside the sea terminal where the ships crew takes over to deliver them to your cabin. Boarding is by gangplanks and accommodation ladders in some ports; by jetway-type ramps at the best ports.

Once aboard, the mood is festive; champagne flowing, all flags flying, the band playing. In your cabin, a welcome-aboard package with all the essential information you will need for life aboard: the who, what, where, and when of everything.

Most public rooms are accessible, but the movies sometimes are not nor are some lounges and discos. Activities often touch on some arts and crafts, with other lectures on living, business or finances, and on the history or theme of the cruise. Samplings of the gentlemanly types of sports are common: swimming, tennis, golf, skeet shooting, and spas.

Games of skill (bridge, chess, backgammon, etc.) and games of chance abound. In the casino, slots, craps, blackjack, roulette, etc. For a slower pace, bingo, anchor pools, dummy horse races, and 1000-piece jigsaw puzzles. Or one can sun, doze, day-dream, gaze, or just socialize.

Many similar activities and services are found aboard the large super ferries of today. Smaller river and canal barges settle for quieter pastimes letting other guests and the proximate shore be the primary attractions.

Dining

Large ferries and cruise ships have many dining choices: buffets, grill, snack bars, and specialty cuisines. Room service is often available.

Luxury-plus ships may have open seating. Others have one or two dinner seatings, with two to eight persons at a table, smoking or non-smoking. The evening dinner's first seating is usually at 6:00 PM and at 8 to 10 PM for the second seating. Correspondingly, there is an early show at 8 PM and a late one following at 10 PM.

Wheelchair persons should advise the maitre d' of the wheelchair at the time of indicating their preferences of table size and seating time. He will assign a table near the entrance for easier access. If dissatisfied with your dining arrangements (or companions), he will change your table but only if the change is made before the third night out.

Elevators

The large, new ships all have 36" to 42" wide elevator doors to handle the traffic, but the doors of smaller, older ships may only have 26" to 28" openings and are barely long enough to carry a single wheelchair.

If the elevators are jammed at dinner time from a pre-dinner reception or cocktail party on a higher deck, ride the empty one on its way back up to be first aboard for its return down to the dining room.

Farewell Dinner and Show

A grand farewell dinner brings showy desserts such as Baked Alaska or Cherries Jubilee. The most talented crew members then make up the after-dinner show. It is a fun show, often the best of the week. Unleashed after a week of servility, the youthful crew members plunge into their native dances and songs with a wholesomeness, gusto, and spontaneity that is refreshing and a delight to watch.

Gift Shops

Good selections of better merchandise are all there to tempt you including the latest sportswear and fashions, jewelry and perfumes. Sundry shops have souvenirs, cards, some paperbacks, etc.

Information / News

Daily notices delivered to your cabins summarize daily shipboard activities as well as world events. Many cabins now also have TV's. Course and position are updated and prominently displayed on charts.

Library

Books are usually borrowed on the honor system. Welcome donations include travel, mystery, classic, and current best sellers.

Lifeboat Drill

Drills are mandated within 24 hours of going to sea. Life jackets are kept either in a locker at your muster station or are placed under the bed or in a closet in your cabin. Check access to that muster station on Promenade Deck in advance. If it is not accessible, contact a ship's officer.

Mail

Letters may be posted at the Purser's Office; foreign stamps are sometimes available there too. Incoming mail goes to your stateroom.

Mal de Mer

Anti-roll stabilizers, fair sailing areas, and good times of the year all help, but occasional rough weather early on a trip will put many to the test. Anti-motion sickness pills, such as Dramamine, Bonine, Antivert, or Marezine, help for a few hours. Some travelers claim an acupuncture-based Sea Band wrist strap is effective while ginger root and garlic is the cure-all for others. For longer periods, prescription Transderm patches placed behind the ear may be effective for three days (if needed, the ship's doctor will renew the prescription for a small fee).

Others get their sea legs by getting out on deck when the ship first leaves port. It's an exciting time. View the passing scene: the ships, the coast, or the horizon (but not the water below). And eat a good meal. It settles your stomach. After that, you'll roll with the best of the old salts.

Medical Services

A small sick bay and well stocked pharmacy with a doctor and nurse present are commonly found aboard cruise ships. Many ships also have helicopter landing pads topside for emergency evacuation if the ship is near better shore facilities.

Money Exchange

Dollars are welcome in most well-visited ports. Money exchanges can also frequently be made at the Purser's Office, or by bank representatives who come aboard in some ports. Exchange rates change daily, but they are listed on the business pages of daily newspapers; the *Wall Street Journal* lists 50 world currency rates daily, and *USA Today*, 23 of them.

Passports and Visas

Your advance trip packet will advise you of any special requirements. Once aboard, only your boarding pass is needed to go ashore and reboard.

Pets

The *Queen Elizabeth 2* carries a kennel, but most other ships ban pets. Blind persons must travel with an able seeing companion, who may also serve as a guide for three or four others, as sometimes arranged for by some of the travel agencies specializing in handicapped travel.

Photographs

The Ship's Photographer covers major events and will respond to any reasonable request. Photos are prominently displayed for potential purchase.

Purser's Office

All money matters are handled here, including the settlement of final bills, stamp purchases, etc.

Religious Services

Catholic, Protestant, and Jewish services are held on most ships with notices provided in the daily activity announcement sheets.

Safe Deposit Boxes

A few ships have such safes in the staterooms, but on most others, they are available only in the Purser's Office.

Ship-to-Shore Communications

Telephone anywhere in the world from your stateroom. Satellite communications include FAX, TELEX, telegrams sent and received.

U.S. Customs

If you are out of the country for 48 hours, $400/person is duty free. So too are antiques (over 100 years old), one quart of alcohol, 100 cigars (even Cuban if bought there) and 200 cigarettes. Duty is 10% from $400 to $1000 unless the products came from the U.S. Virgin Islands, Guam, or American Samoa. Then the duty exemption rises to $800, with no more than $400 spent outside these islands. One gallon of alcohol (or 1000 cigarettes and 100 cigars) can be brought from these islands duty free, but only one quart of alcohol can be from outside these islands.

Visitors in Ports Visited

Arrange for visits ahead of time; security is a concern.

Wine and Alcoholic Beverages

Alcoholic beverages are available. The Wine Steward will chill and pour your wine, and also store unfinished (?) potions for the next meal.

FOREIGN PORTS OF CALL

Itineraries should be checked to ensure many dockside landings, but berths are sometimes taken and one must often anchor at smaller ports.

Tendering

When anchoring, ships always retain the right to deny you passage ashore. In calm weather, however, the Captain may authorize it.

Husky crewmen must lift you and your chair bodily for the descent down the accommodation ladder to board the small, bobbing, rolling shore boat. Last to board (usually alongside the boat's coxswain), you will be the first off. Other passengers crowd below on narrow seats.

If you stay aboard, there is still much to do. You can socialize with others who may have visited the port before, or who, like you, chose to stay aboard. The staff will give you more attention. The lounges and decks will be uncrowded. A most relaxing day.

Shore Excursions‖

Shore excursions planned by the Tour Office are generally not accessible to the physically handicapped. The Tour Director will give a talk on the port to be visited the day before arrival; maps of the city identifying major points of interest are available from the Tour Office.

For towns, try a walking (rolling) tour if near the center of town, or a short taxi ride there. To match the ship's tour, hire a taxi or private guide (whose English you understand) that are found waiting at every port.

We have found the cost of these private tours to be no greater than the planned ship's tour for two people. You will save half the cost of the tour with another couple. Better yet, you can tailor your tour to your liking: two hours, half a day, or all day. In this way, both your time and the driver's are spent more efficiently and pleasantly. You have a wider choice of dining areas, and things to do.

DISEMBARKING

Disembarkment information is distributed, and a talk explaining the procedure given by the Cruise Director, the day before arrival. Except for a small hand-carried bag, other bags are tagged and left in the passageway for pickup on the evening before arrival.

Travelers are expected to have settled their accounts at the Purser's Office that morning or the evening before. Any tips or gratuities should also have been dispensed the previous evening or that morning, or should be left in an envelope for the individual at the Purser's Office. It's "off with your head" if you try to tip an officer.

When cleared by customs and immigration, disembarkation takes place in groups dependent on the time urgency of travel connections.

Once on shore, you will find your tagged bags by ship's deck number, alphabetically arranged by last name. Porters will be handy. A valet can bring your car around. Now, there are but letters to write, photos to develop, bills to pay, and time to dream and plan anew.

APPENDIXES

APPENDIX A
ADAPTING WHEELCHAIRS

An inch, my kingdom for an inch! Openings always a little too narrow, and the wheelchair too wide.

Children's seat widths are 14"; those for youth and adults are 15" to 22", with 18" being most common. That is not too bad; doorways are wider. But wheelchairs are almost 50% wider. The wheel hubs and arm rests add another 8" to 9" to the overall width. The resulting width of 24" to 28" is too great for most cabins and all but a few especially modified wheelchair accessible bathrooms.

Where do those extra inches come from and is there anything to be done to shrink them? First the large wheel itself. The hub and a half-inch spacer add 3" to each side to yield six of those inches. Spoked wheels need an extra half inch over molded wheels for the same lateral strength. Sports chairs with tilted wheels add still other inches for the camber. Space for the wheel to clear the arm rests on some chairs make up the remainder of those inches.

Figure A-1 illustrates the problem. The large wheel must clear the frame and skirt guard of the arm rest. The front of the arm rest is clear of the wheel, but if the arm rest's rear bracket is also mounted outboard of the frame, the wheel must move out another 3/4" on each side to clear the arm rest. A welded spacer is added to the main frame's axle support to provide this clearance for the wheels.

"Wrap-a-round" **hinged,** removable (or folding) arm rests, however, have their bracket mounted behind the vertical main frame. They do not

Figure A-1

Factors affecting wheelchair widths.

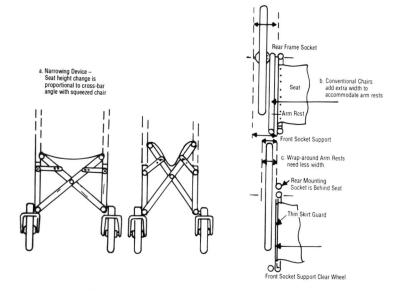

a. Narrowing Device –
Seat height change is
proportional to cross-bar
angle with squeezed chair

Rear Frame Socket

b. Conventional Chairs
add extra width to
accommodate arm rests

Seat

Arm Rest

Front Socket Support

c. Wrap-around Arm Rests
need less width.

Rear Mounting
Socket is Behind Seat

Thin Skirt Guard

Front Socket Support Clear Wheel

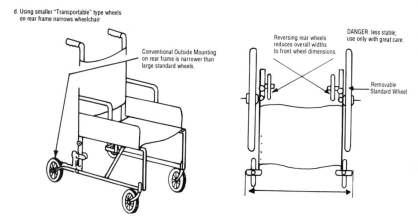

d. Using smaller "Transportable" type wheels
on rear frame narrows wheelchair

Conventional Outside Mounting
on rear frame is narrower than
large standard wheels.

Reversing rear wheels
reduces overall widths
to front wheel dimensions

DANGER: less stable;
use only with great care.

Removable
Standard Wheel

add extra inches to clear the wheel and are more than an inch narrower than those on conventional chairs.

Some sports chairs (i.e., the "Quickie") have fold-down arms with no skirt guards, but their canted wheels (used for better cornering) still end up adding 9" to the overall chair's width by adding 1.5" for every 3° of camber.

The narrowest chairs are the "transportable" type that use only small wheels mounted underneath the seat, much like a stroller. Sometimes rented for cruises, such chairs are typically 22.5" wide which is still 4" to 5" wider than the seat width itself. The disadvantage is that the user loses the ability to wheel and control the chair himself.

Narrower still are the aisle chairs of some airlines. In Paris and Tokyo, for example, both the brackets for the front caster wheels and the small rear wheels are each welded to the **inside** of the frame. The chair width becomes no wider than the seat itself, i.e., less than 18" overall. Pivoted arm rests are bolted to the outside of the frame to clear the aisle seats, but a wrap-around arm rest design would eliminate that interference and leave the overall width no greater than that of the seat itself.

Except for the sills described in the pages ahead, such chairs would be accessible almost anywhere, but with the wheels closer together, the chairs are less stable laterally.

Wheelchair-using cruise travelers therefore have four choices for getting into their cabin or bathroom; (1) book one of the many ships with accessible cabins noted in PARTS I, II and III, (2) rent a narrower chair as described above, (3) transfer to a stool at the entrance and slide through, or (4), if the interference is small, attempt to temporarily narrow the chair as described below

How To Narrow An Existing Chair

Two ways to narrow an existing chair are to somehow squeeze it together, or to find some temporary substitute for those large hubbed wheels.

Some limitations, but squeezing is simple. As shown in Figure A-1, the seat and two side frame supports are connected by a scissors or camp-stool-like crossbar. Squeeze them together, the seat rises, but the overall width becomes less. If the crossbars are at a 45° angle, for small changes, the height increases proportionally to the width reduction.

We have found that a small lateral push often just clears a small interference, but for greater interferences, more dramatic solutions are needed.

Everest & Jennings has an optional hugger attachment called "Reduce-a-Width" and until recently, Activeaid, Inc. of Redwood Fall, Minnesota, marketed a simple pulley system for squeezing the chair together, but it has since abandoned the product.

J.T. Gillum Sr. of Gainesville, Florida has similarly sold pulley devices to narrow chairs several inches while simultaneously raising the seat a like amount. He has been working with a couple of engineers on an electric hydraulic one too through Professional Service Unlimited.

The other alternative is to substitute the large wheels forming such a large part of the overall width of a chair for the smaller wheels found in transportable chairs. Knowledgeable John Wilkinson of Home Medical Equipment, Fort Myers, FL, pointed out that the rear-wheel assemblies of Invacare's transportable chairs were designed to just slip onto the frame of a conventional chair. The cost of a pair of such wheels is a fraction of the cost of a separate chair. Quick-release main wheels makes the switch over even easier.

The narrowed chairs are good enough in the confines of a stateroom, and sometimes the aisle of an airplane, but like the aisle chairs described earlier, they are not as laterally stable as those with more widely spaced wheels; an able companion should be near at hand.

We therefore carry the small wheels along in our bags when traveling extensively in uncharted waters. On some chairs, the wheels can even be slipped onto the inside of the tilt bars if they just clear the ground. The small wheels must be removed for storage however, but otherwise they are handy and out of the way.

Narrower chairs solve many of the problems of older ships, but sills and occasional steps remain the biggest blocks aboard ship.

Sills, Steps, and Ramps

Everything's not on the level. The ADA act (Appendix B) recommends a rise of one inch per foot, a 5° angle. That seems modest enough. Mountain highways have runaway truck escape routes when 5° grade warning signs are posted. Grades for ramps longer than 32' are recommended to be 1 to 16.

Most ramps, and gangways certainly, far exceed that standard, but they're better than curbs. Narrow ledges or sills are worst of all.

Figure A-2 illustrates the problem. It is easy to climb a simple step or curb by tilting the chair backward and using the leverage of the chair against the front wheel to climb a curb (a wheelie). Reverse order for descending a curb (or steep ramp) by backing down.

Sills are a problem whichever way they are approached. Putting the front wheels over the sill is no problem (unless the sill is so high, or wide, the chair doesn't clear and gets hung up on the frame instead). But raising the rear wheels to the top of the sill tips the person forward making him want to slide, or fall out of the chair. The angles aren't small; climbing a "small" 4" sill tilts the chair forward 17°, a 6" inch sill almost 30°.

As in climbing stairs, tilting the chair backwards and backing up keeps the person in the chair, but the leverage is wrong for a single companion to brake the crash coming down from the top of the sill. Two persons are therefore needed to first lift and then brake the fall on the other side. The alternative is to have a temporary ramp made up by the ship's carpenter for your private bathroom if not so equipped.

For climbing or descending stairs, one or preferably two strong people are needed at each end of the chair. It is best for the wheelchair person to always faces down the stairs (whether climbing or descending) with the chair tilted back and the wheel touching the edges of one or two steps to carry some of the load. Sometimes ship's crew members will insist on carrying you backwards even on a descent. This is most unnerving since it imposes an extraordinarily difficult and awkward handling problem for themselves.

Figure A-2

Single steps are simple; sills are difficult unless physically lifted over them .

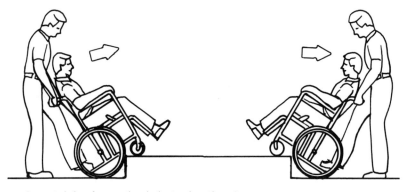

Proper technique for mounting single steps is not hazardous.

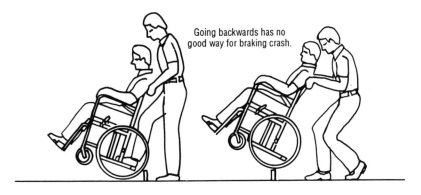

Going backwards has no good way for braking crash.

Sills are hazardous unless physically lifted over them.

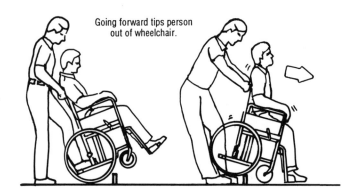

Going forward tips person out of wheelchair.

Figure A-3
Ramps and Steps.

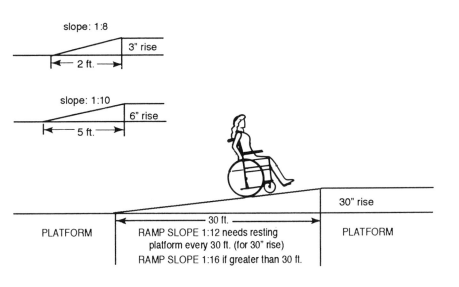

slope: 1:8
3" rise
2 ft.

slope: 1:10
6" rise
5 ft.

30" rise

PLATFORM

30 ft.
RAMP SLOPE 1:12 needs resting
platform every 30 ft. (for 30" rise)
RAMP SLOPE 1:16 if greater than 30 ft.

PLATFORM

We have found it best to face down the steps
when climbing or descending stairs.

APPENDIX B
AMERICANS WITH DISABILITIES ACT

Revised sections covering the transport of handicapped persons were proposed by the U.S. Department of Transportation on 4 April 1991 with hearings scheduled through the summer. Primary attention was given to terminals or stations, commuter routes, and other commonly used transportation methods used by able persons for ordinary living.

A standard wheelchair space allowance of 30" by 48" was established as a reference to allow some knuckle and toe clearances beyond the nominal 26" wide by 42" long dimensions of a standard chair. A minimum width of 32" was defined for door or jamb openings, long passageways or halls, were to be 3' wide to allow room for turning into a doorway. Elsewhere, 5' diameter turning circles were specified.

In bathrooms, water closet stall doors were to open outward to allow the wheelchair person to close the door behind him. For bathing, 3' square shower stalls or bathtubs with 30" adjacent clearance were also specified.

Excepting river boats, canal barges, and some extraordinarily stable ships like the *Radisson Diamond* ships need some type of sill to contain the water in a shower. Hence sills are common, but often ramped for the handicapped.

Ramp slopes were set at a rise of 1 in 12 for runs of less than 30', and 1 to 16 for longer runs. That is not unreasonable on solid earth, but it is a problem aboard ship.

Any of several decks may be used for embarkation, but changing tides, river levels, or a ship's loading must match the 10 foot deck level variation. Conforming to the 1 to 16 ADA slope requirement would result in an impractical 160 ft. long ramp to be stored aboard ship with rest platforms along the way. Ashore, elevators, Jetways, and sometimes forklift-type aids can easily accommodate a changing platform height level, but it is a problem at less developed ports. But wherever, able crewmen are always at hand at the gangway to aid passengers. Special attention from several courteous, strong young sailors is not that bad and one must accept that means of going ashore abroad anyway.

Extracts from the proposed guidelines for ferries and other boats or ships are presented below followed in turn by a short section on air travel which is most commonly used for the fly/cruise packages.

Ferries, Excursion Boats & Other Vehicles

The Federal Register, Volume 56, No. 65, included only the following few words in Paragraph 177 of Section I on Other Vehicles and Systems.

"(a) Doorways. Doorways to all passenger areas shall have a minimum clear opening of 32 inches. Thresholds may be a maximum 3/4 inch to accommodate gaskets and water seals provided they are beveled on both sides."

"(b) Seating Areas. At least one area for passengers using wheelchairs or mobility aids shall be provided as close as practicable to an accessible entrance, and adjacent to seating of other passengers, with a clear floor area of 30 inches by 48 inches. Not more than 6 inches of the required clear floor space may be accommodated for footrests under another seat provided there is a minimum of 9 inches from the floor to the lowest part of the seat overhanging the space. Such areas may have fold-down seats to accommodate other passengers when a wheelchair or mobility aid is not occupying the area provided the seats, when folded up, do not obstruct the clear floor space required."

"(c) Securement. [Reserved]."

"(d) Gangplanks. Gangplanks and other boarding devices shall comply with 125(c)."

"(e) Restrooms. If restrooms are provided for the general public they shall comply with 123(a), (1) through (5), and shall be connected to the seating area(s) required by paragraph (b) of this section by an unobstructed route at least 32 inches wide."

"(f) Elevators. [Reserved]."

Section 123(a) on restrooms specifies clear floor areas of 35 by 60 inches, water closet heights between 17 and 19 inches, grab bars, faucets and controls no more than 44 inches above the floor, and a doorway opening of 32 inches.

Section 125(c) on ramps speaks of no protrusions greater than a 1/4 inch, a clear width of 30 inches, 2 inch high barrier guards on either side or edge of the ramp, and slopes 1:8 for 3 inch riseor 1:10 for a 6 inch rise.

Air Travel Carrier Summary Rules for Handicapped Passengers

The salient rules are listed below for only U.S. New aircraft requirements are for those newly ordered or delivered within two years of the order. No extra charges can be levied as a result of any of these accommodations.

1. "New aircraft (30 or more seats) must have the movable aisle arm rests on half the aisles in the aircraft."

2. "New widebody aircraft must have accessible bathrooms."

3. "New aircraft (100 or more seats) must have priority space for storing a wheelchair in the cabin."

4. "Aircraft (60 or more seats) with accessible lavatory must have an on-board chair. For flights on aircraft that do not have accessible lavatories, handicapped passengers who can use an inaccessible lavatory but need an on-board wheelchair to reach the lavatory can, with 48 hours advance notice, have an on-board wheelchair on their flight."

Carriers may not refuse transportation of the handicapped unless they provide a written explanation based solely on flight safety, nor can they require an attendant unless they provide free transport for the attendant in cases of disagreement of whether one is required.

No seat is excluded because of a handicap except on exit rows where the FAA allows carriers to place only passengers who can perform the functions necessary in an emergency evacuation.

When preboarding, wheelchairs and aids have priority storage over items boarded at the same airport by other passengers. Other items must comply with FAA's carry-on baggage rules.

Carriers must also accept battery-powered vehicles and, if necessary, package the batteries in hazardous materials boxes that they provide.

APPENDIX C
SHIPS, BOATS, AND STUFF

First, a few things encountered aboard ship and for finding your way at sea. Then a bit more on boats and ships (all types), later on in this Appendix.

Ships and boats. Excepting the Nordic "bot" and the Navy's "pigboats," boats are small. Small boats are used for fishing, rowing, racing or paddling about. Ships are larger; they carry boats as tenders or as lifeboats. But a river boat is a boat, and except in France, a canal barge a barge.

Ship's Gear

Essential things are shown first in Figure C-1. Gangplanks bridge the gap between ship and shore from any one of several decks having side opening doors. Pierside, the gangway is mounted on rollers to facilitate the slide along the pier or wharf from the changing ramp angle as the loading of the ship or tides change.

There is often a short, steep ramp to a big step at the gangway's dockside end, and a short steeper ramp from the top of the gangway where it enters the ship to the nearby deck. Crew members are always there to help, however. Better yet, some well equipped cruise terminals have motorized boarding ramps similar to the jetways at major airports.

Getting ashore from an anchorage is a bigger problem. An accommodation ladder is lowered to the waters edge from one of the higher decks. As shown in Figure C-1, the height of the ladder's lower boarding platform is adjusted for the best level of the tender or shore boat then being used. In sheltered harbors, crew members may carry you in your chair down (and later up) these steps, and onto the shore boat if you cannot walk. Some cruise lines flatly refuse to do so as a matter of policy. Others are more accommodating, but it is always at the discretion of the Captain.

Except when abandoning ship; no choice then! Boarding is actually easier, however. The lifeboats are lowered even with the Promenade Deck before boarding and then lowered into the water below. A listing

Figure C-1
Standard and Emergency Ship Access

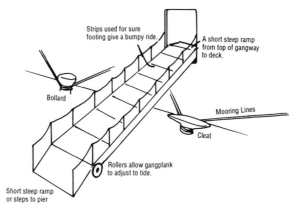

Strips used for sure footing give a bumpy ride.

A short steep ramp from top of gangway to deck.

Bollard

Mooring Lines

Cleat

Rollers allow gangplank to adjust to tide.

Short steep ramp or steps to pier

Typical Dockside Boarding Gangway

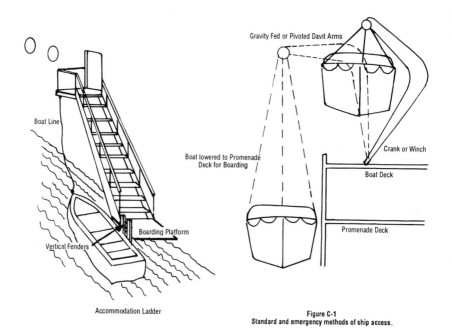

Boat Line

Boarding Platform

Vertical Fenders

Accommodation Ladder

Gravity Fed or Pivoted Davit Arms

Crank or Winch

Boat Deck

Boat lowered to Promenade Deck for Boarding

Promenade Deck

Figure C-1
Standard and emergency methods of ship access.

ship perhaps, but no bobbing boat.

A rare occasion, but it does happen, like on the *Prinsendam* after an engine fire forced abandonment of its repositioning journey back to the Orient from Alaska. The orderly abandonment, with all passengers and crew saved, speaks well of the disciplined Dutch officers and crew, and the good and thorough lifeboat drill they had conducted earlier.

Another happy ending, but no thanks to the ship's captain in the small ship that sank in a storm off of Africa. Ordering abandon ship, he reportedly pushed his way past the passengers to be one of the first off. (Chartered, the hotel staff stayed and did a fine job helping the passengers first, however.) That insensitivity of the captain, may not be too surprising since he belonged to a line with NO handicapped cabins in any of its ships!

The lifeboats themselves are motorized, with sealed buoyancy tanks to keep the boat afloat even if swamped. There are enough of them on board for all passengers with seats to spare, but not for all the crew. In an emergency, they take to one of the large number of liferafts on board.

Lifeboats on the Boat Deck are mounted on davits for easy lowering to the Promenade Deck below. Davit designs vary, but most are gravity types that can operate when all power fails. When released, the boat cradles roll down the inclined tracks and out even with the side before being lowered to the deck below.

Ship Navigation and Piloting

Plotting your position within sight of land is called piloting; when at sea, it is called navigation.

Shooting the stars in the evening and measuring noon sun lines have largely given way to the new space and electronic age technologies. Ships now determine their position anywhere in the world to a few hundred feet by accurately measuring the time of arrival of radio signals from different orbiting navigation satellites.

Other systems determine their position by comparing the precise time of arrival of simultaneously broadcast radio signals from three or more ground stations.

LORAN C, one such system with a range of about 600 miles from shore (or 200 miles under good ionospheric radio conditions), is used extensively around the United States, North Atlantic, and the Pacific. DECCA is a shorter-range system used around Japan, Europe, and South Africa. Still another worldwide, but less accurate low-frequency system, OMEGA, is often used as a backup.

Closer to shore, piloting uses line-of-sight triangulation between known landmarks or navigational aids near shore. When returning to port, buoys marking harbor entrances are red on the starboard side, and green on the port; hence the easy to remember phrase, "Red, Right, Returning."

Lights are used to identify potential hazards and to give some indication of the ship's heading when it is underway. The colored bow lights for the first 10 points (see Appendix D) are red for port (like port wine) and green for starboard, which, together with two, 32-point white masthead lights (the lower one forward), provide a rough estimate of direction. Starboard is to the right when facing forward, because Norsemen who used steering boards ("staerboards") on the side of their boats were right-handed. Keeping the "staerboard" outboard and free to use, "port" was the side to which you tied up to in port. Some others with shorter memories, or with a more limited vocabulary, note that both "left" and "port" are four letter words.

Masthead lights are white over red for the Pilot Boat, red over white for line or drift fishermen, green over white for trawlers, etc., etc.

Other pre-Marconi signals include flags and whistles. For flags, red "B" is for refueling, the red and white striped "H" for pilot aboard, the yellow "Q" for quarantine, etc.

Whistles signal changes to another vessel. On approach, one long blast is a course change to starboard, two blasts to port, three blasts stopped and four blasts, backing down.

Ship Design

As with other large structures, the hull itself is framed. Transverse and longitudinal frames are mounted from the main structural backbone of the ship, the keelson, and strengthened further with steel plates.

Figure C-2
Ship (Hull) Design Elements.

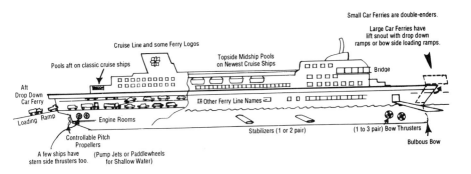

Small Car Ferries are double-enders.

Large Car Ferries have lift snout with drop down ramps or bow side loading ramps.

Cruise Line and some Ferry Logos

Pools aft on classic cruise ships

Topside Midship Pools on Newest Cruise Ships

Bridge

Aft Drop Down Car Ferry

Loading Ramp

Engine Rooms

☒ Other Ferry Line Names ☒

Stabilizers (1 or 2 pair)

(1 to 3 pair) Bow Thrusters

Bulbous Bow

Controllable Pitch Propellers

A few ships have stern side thrusters too.

(Pump Jets or Paddlewheels for Shallow Water)

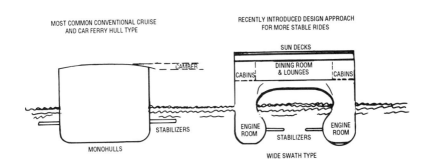

MOST COMMON CONVENTIONAL CRUISE AND CAR FERRY HULL TYPE

RECENTLY INTRODUCED DESIGN APPROACH FOR MORE STABLE RIDES

SUN DECKS

DINING ROOM & LOUNGES

CABINS

CABINS

CAMBER

STABILIZERS

ENGINE ROOM

STABILIZERS

ENGINE ROOM

MONOHULLS

WIDE SWATH TYPE

HIGH SPEED LIGHT CAPACITY HULL FORMS (Usually Passsenger Only Ferries)

AIR SKIRTS

SURFACE EFFECT AND PLANING HULLS

FOILS

HYDRO AND JETFOILS

HOVERCRAFT OR AIR CUSHION VESSELS

The highest full deck running from stem to stern is the Main Deck; below it, the ship is compartmented with watertight bulkheads and decks to contain any potential hull damage.

Since days of yore, all ships have had a high prow for the bow waves and high stem for following seas. Lighter boats in calmer waters could be long and slender, but as illustrated in Figure C-2, for heavier cargo a squat midships was needed for stability. Sheer was the rise of decks towards either bow or stern; camber, the whale back curve across the deck to shed water.

Over the years, the length-to-beam ratio has varied little, but not the freeboard, mechanical aids, propulsion and overall size of ships. With ever more powerful engines, new shapes have evolved in recent years to speed the journey.

Contrasting with the West's early use of steering boards (as noted above), the Chinese long ago invented the centerline rudder for better maneuverability on their cramped rivers.

Today other new mechanically controlled devices appear. Like pre-jet airplanes, the ship's main propellers are now variable or controllable-pitch-types to permit quick reversal in tight quarters without having to arrest the inertia of those massive blades. As on the *Radisson Diamond*, some of them are mounted in cowlings that swivel to direct the thrust in any direction, not unlike that of an outboard engine.

Found in the bow of many cruise ships are bow thrusters, while a few also have stern thrusters. With the thrust directed laterally, they're used to translate the bow of the ship from one side to the other to change heading in tight quarters or even when dead in the water.

Stabilizers are now commonly used on cruise and large open sea ferries to dampen the ship's rolling motions. Not unlike an airplane's ailerons, one or two pairs of large fins or foils project outward, tilting their lift angles to oppose the ship's rolling motions. With gyroscopes instantly sensing motions, and correcting them automatically with their fins, the ships can dampen as much as 90% of a normal roll when underway.

Stability

Ever wonder why a ship floats upright? The center of gravity is certainly higher than the underwater center of buoyancy. Isn't it like a top balancing on its point? Yes, but ...

As the ship rolls, the increased immersed volume on one side of the ship, adds to the buoyancy of that side, subtracting an equal amount from the other to shift the center of buoyancy to the immersed side. If that shift is greater than any corresponding shift of the center of gravity. the ship will right itself. If not, it capsizes. Hence the great pains given to prevent free-running water from shifting the center of gravity to the lowered side.

Naval architects define the intersection of the vertical line passing through the center of buoyancy with the ship level and when it is heeled over, as the metacenter. For a ship to remain stable, the metacenter must remain above the center of gravity. The distance between the c.g. and the metacenter (the metacentric height), is a critical measure of stability.

To a first approximation, it is one fifth the square of the ship's breadth or beam (in feet) divided by the square of the ship's characteristic roll period in seconds. If that roll period (not roll angle) increases significantly, there is cause for alarm and action.

An Unconventional Design

Invented by a Canadian 50 years ago, the SWATH (Small Waterplane Area Twin Hull) type ships provide exceptional stability for larger displacement ships. Two large, deeply submerged hulls provide most of the buoyancy. The waterline area of the necked-down structures that support the upper decks is small, and hence waves do not have as great a disturbing action as an equivalent monohull.

With double the underwater wetted-surface area of these ships compared to monohulls, they are slower for the same sized propulsion plant. They hold this speed in rough weather better, however, than does a rolling, regularly hulled ship hold its speed. Naval ASW vessels needing a more level plarform to listen to underwater sounds, and some small ferries benefiting from the wide deck areas for their light cargo, are built this way, as is the *Radisson Diamond* described below.

The exceptionally wide beam and small waterline allows very stable sea going qualities. Contrasting with other ships, fixed (not retractable) stabilizers project inward between the two hulls. Overall, the design is more spacious, with less roll than even the very largest of ocean liners.

The top deck is a grand expanse of open area for all. Below, all of the stateroom suites are aligned outboard, along each side of the wide hull, with large picture windows and many private outboard verandas. Between the staterooms on the lower decks are conference rooms, theatre, and a spacious lounge with three-deck high windows facing forward. A large, uncrowded, single-seating dining room with two-deck high grand windows face aft. (A hydraulically lowered built-in marina between the hulls is not accessible for the handicapped.)

Maneuverability is excellent. Bow thrusters can translate the bow in either direction, while aft, controllable cowlings around the controllable-pitch propellers allow thrust in any direction. The ship can translate sideways in either direction, or spin on a dime when stopped.

Speed and Drag

A ship's resistance is comprised of (1), wetted-surface area drag and (2), at higher speeds, a much greater bow wave making resistance. Large conventional monohulls reduce this latter factor by use of the large underwater, bulbous bows shown in Figure C-2.

Discovered accidentally by the Navy at the beginning of this century, it was observed that the older, battering-ram warships were more seaworthy and faster than their newer sleek-bowed ones. The early pressure from the underwater projection anticipates and reduces the large bow wave and its contribution to the ship's drag. It is found on every major, deep-water vessel today.

At high speeds, the biggest drag factor for all boats is their inherent bow-wave making characteristics. To minimize that factor, the fastest boats lift the bulk of their weight up out of the water through one of three techniques illustrated in Figure C-2 : (1), a set of underwater foils or wings (hydrofoil or, if by a jet engine, jetfoil), (2), floating it on a cushion of air (hovercraft), or (3), a planing hull capitalizing on the water's surface tension characteristics.

APPENDIX D
WINDS AND WAVES

The sea is three fourths of the world's surface. If the mountains were scraped into the deep ocean trenches, that's all we'd see, the sea.

As for the waves, the longer the body of open water (the fetch) and the brisker and longer the wind blows over it (the duration), the bigger the waves. Ripples start in light air, 1 to 3 knots; scattered whitecaps develop at 7 to 10 knots (8 to 12 mph) and so on up to the giant waves of hurricanes.

Heights of waves are measured from trough to top, lengths from crest to crest. Fresh violent storms have ratios of 10 to 1 for length to height, older ones, 40 to 1, but on the average they're 20 to 1. In extreme cases, hurricanes bring waves a thousand feet long and over 150 feet high.

A violent storm or hurricane needs the fetch and time duration to develop, several thousand miles, and several days at least, time enough for most ships to head for safer waters, warned by the ever-present overhead weather satellites.

It wasn't always so. Early seamen used their eyes to judge wind and the weather. Without modern instruments, their best call on wind velocity was the appearance of the sea's surface. Becalmed with winds less than one knot, the surface had a glassy appearance. Light airs (1 to 3 knots) brought on ripples in the water, gentle breezes brought crests that were just beginning to break, moderate, fresh, and strong breezes brought larger waves and foam, and on to gales, storms, and hurricanes.

The Beaufort Scale listed in Table D-1 is a shorthand method for describing wind conditions. Glassy ocean conditions became Force 0, light air was Force 1, etc., all based on a logarithmic scale.

Weather forecasting in the tropics varied little from today's announcers, "light to variable winds, scattered afternoon showers." More telling was the sailor's weather eye on cloud formations, the tell tale cirrus from a coming front. And equally accurate was the sky's color at dawn or dusk: "Red sky at morn, sailor be warned; red sky at night, sailor's delight."

Table D

Beaufort Scale and Winds and Wave

	Wind Speed			Ocean's Surface	Average Wave (ft)		
Force	knots	mph	Descriptor	Appearance	Height (1)	(2)	Length
0	0-1	0-1	Calm	Glassy, like a mirror.	0		0
1	1-3	1-3	Light air	Ripples on surface, like a fish scale.	0.1		1
2	4-6	4-7	Light breeze	Small wavelets; crests don't break	0.2		7
3	7-10	8-12	Gentle breeze	Large wavelets and scattered whitecaps.	0.6	2	20
4	11-16	13-18	Moderate breeze	Small waves, frequent whitecaps.	2	3.5	50
5	17-21	18-24	Fresh breeze	Moderate waves, many whitecaps.	4	6	100
6	22-27	25-31	Strong breeze	Large waves; white foam crests common.	8	9.5	160
7	28-33	32-38	High wind	White foam in streaks	14	13.5	260
8	34-40	39-46	Fresh gale	Moderately high waves; streaking foam.	23	18	380
9	41-47	47-54	Strong gale	High waves; rolling sea	36	23	530
10	48-55	55-63	Storm	Very high waves, curling crests, visibility affected	50	29	700
11	56-63	64-73	Violent storm	Huge waves, froth and foam everywhere	73	37	1000
12	>63	>73	Hurricane	Poor visibility, all-white driving spray.	>80	45	>1000

(1) Fully risen sea.

(2) Average wave

Calling the Directions

With no accurate gyroscopes to aid them, ancient mariners called directions from the heading of the ship or from the magnetic compass. Thirty two "points" (11.25°) were as close as they could call a direction or steer a ship. North, South, East and West were the four primary ones, and combinations of those cardinal points for four others, NE, NW, SE, and SW. The next eight split those earlier headings, i.e. NNE, ENE, ESE, SSE, etc. The final 16 split the earlier 16 headings by adding a "by": North by East, Northeast by North, Northeast by East, East by North, etc. The first 8 points of the compass then became N, N by E, NNE, NE by N, NE, NE by E, ENE, E by N, E etc.

GLOSSARY OF
NAUTICAL TERMS

a-: (or "ab-" if followed by vowel as in abaft) sailor's shorthand for all prepositions and articles (most often followed by a place or direction as in aboard, alee, amidships, aport, ashore, athwart etc.).

A.B.: able bodied, as in able-bodied seaman.

accommodation ladder: a ladder carried aboard ship for lowering from upper deck to dockside or the waters edge.

aft: direction to stern or rear of boat or ship.

anchor: heavy object resting on, or buried in a seabed with flukes to which a line or chain is secured to limit ship's drift. Contrast with moor or mooring which uses two or more lines.

anchorage: the water area used for anchoring (also road).

ballast: added weight for stability or trimming ship; also mother-in-law who came along at the last minute.

barge: a large flat-bottomed boat for carrying heavy cargo; in the Navy, a boat for carrying wide-bottomed admirals.

beam: the wide part of a ship; its width.

below: any enclosed area if topside, a lower deck if already below.

biddy: one of those abominally narrow staterooms aboard cruise ships with porthole at one end; also an abominably gossipy woman at your table you dislike almost as much as yourself for not asking the maitre d' to change your table once again.

binnacle: housing for magnetic compass with large iron navigator's balls to compensate for magnetic deviation.

bitter end: the far end of a long line; also paying the bills after returning home.

block: wood or metal frame containing pulleys; "to block" is to bring a load up against the block; as in sills that block wheelchair entries.

block and tackle: roughing it up ashore when pronounced "tack" "ul", but at sea, it's "tay" "kul", a combination of pulleys (block) and lines for lifting loads.

boat: any small vessel or watercraft, often carried on board larger sea-going vessels called ships.

bollard: a rounded mooring post.

bow: the pointy end of a ship.

bow line: (bow as in "bow down", line as in a "fishing line", either with hook attached, or a fanciful yarn) the forward mooring line through the chock or bull nose of the ship.

bowline (pronounced "bow" as in bow tie, and "lin" as in linament): a sailor's favorite non-slip-knot.

breast lines: perpendicular to the ship's centerline, the shortest mooring lines ashore. Ahore, it's what catches a sailor's eye.

bulbous bow: what all deep-draft ships have; spoofing the water into believing it is a larger ship through use of a large, bulbous, underwater bow extending forward of the waterline; it minimizes wave-making resistance.

bulkhead: walls to a seaman.

buoy: moored floats marking submerged objects or boundaries of navigational channels; red buoys to right on entering a harbor (red, right, returning) green ones on left.

cabin: a cabinet-sized stateroom.

camber: the arching of a ship's deck to shed water.

chart: a seaman's map; captains who don't check the small print to see whether depths are marked in feet, fathoms, or meters always run aground. Distance measures are picked off from along <u>vertical, longitude only</u>, scale; one minute of arc equals one nautical mile anywhere in the world. (True too of latitude, but only at the Equator.)

cleat: playing boys' vertical shoe posts or wedges for firmer footing ashore; two large, horizontal horned posts to secure lines for working seaman.

coamings: raised barriers around hatches and other deck openings to block water entry.

coxswain: a small boat's helmsman, pronounced "coxs'n".

cross-staff: long, perpendicular cross stick (staff) used by early seamen to measure star elevations; now a stiffed steward at journey's end.

davits: movable supports for holding and lowering lifeboats at sea.

deck: floor to a sailor.

decked: floored to a sailor.

dead reckoning: navigating blindly without a fix by plotting estimated speed and direction of travel from last fix.

displacement: the true weight of a ship measured by the weight of water it displaces when afloat.

dock: the body of water in which a ship rests when tied up to a pier or wharf, or between two piers.

fathom: average length of seamen's outstretched arm lengths, now 6 feet, used initially for measuring water's depth by length of line attached to stone or lead weight (the lead line) tossed forward until vertical; marks (knots), added for easy counting at night; after adding height of sailor on deck (leadsman) to waterline, the number of knots indicated total length of line to that point as in Mark Twain, two marks, or 12 feet.

flare: the rockets red glare, savoir faire, or spreading of ship's breadth or beam from waterline to main deck.

forward: toward the bow of a boat.

gigs: boats used in the Navy by non-flag officer captains, as in "captain's gig" (Admirals use "barges" . . . they carry more weight).

gross registered tonnage: with certain space exemptions, an obfuscated measure of a ship's enclosed volume. Nominally 100 ft³ per ton, but the definition and factor vary with type and size ship. Interpreted differently by some nations to increase port charges.

gunwale: (pronounced "gun'l") the uppermost edge of boat or ship's side; where guns were once set. See son-of-a-gun.

head: forward part of ship or a toilet; synonymous since sailors once went forward over bowsprits to relieve themselves, while officers used the "poop deck" overhangs aft.

helm: the steering-control mechanism, or the command of same by officer-in-charge, as with General Haig, "I've got the helm".

helmsman: the person with hands-on control of same.

keel: the main structural member running the length of a boat or ship along its bottom.

keel haul: a most unwelcome way of taking a dip in the water; tied up and dragged under a barnacle-encrusted ship for offending the captain, and hence most common.

keel over: too late to head for lifeboats.

keelson: smaller strengthening beams or metal plates attached to the keel inside the vessel for its major structural backbone.

knot: a nautical mile per hour, i.e. a speed or velocity; all those caught saying "knots per hour" are fed to sharks. Term originated by tossing a "log" (a small board) with attached line overboard and counting number of knots that slipped through your fingers in a fixed period of time to calculate the speed.

ladder: "stairs" to a sailor.

Lash: a lighter aboard ship, i.e., a barge carrier; also, until banned by the U.S. Navy in 1862, punishment by flogging with a "cat" of nine tails or a single whip (a "colt") for such heinous offenses as peeing on the quarterdeck from aloft (12 cat lashes).

line: a sailor's rope at sea, or string along with lassies ashore.

load line: the markings near the bow of a ship indicating the maximum ship's loading in fresh or salt water, season of year, etc.

metacenter: the imaginary center through which righting moments pass when the ship heels; the ship will capsize if the metacenter is below the center of gravity.

midships: the fattest part of the ship midway between bow and stern.

nautical mile: 6080.27 feet; also the distance of one minute of arc measured at the earth's circumference, i.e. around it's equator, or along any of its longitudes around the poles; every minute of arc error in star sightings or a 6-microsecond timing error in electronic navigation systems corresponds to a one nautical mile line of position error in fixing a position by triangulation.

navigation: the art of determining one's location at sea away from sight of land; Arabs and other early voyagers invented celestial navigation by measuring elevation angles of stars through astrolabes or cross staffs, later refined by Prince Henry the Navigator of Portugal, and with an accurate watch (chronometer) by England to determine longitude to put a third rate observatory at Greenwich, England on all world maps (charts).

modern navigation: Marconi's legacy; radio direction finding, or measuring the time of arrival of radio broadcasts from known locations of ground stations (LORAN-American, or DECCA English), and now satellites (GPS).

overhead: ceilings at sea.

Panamax: like the QE 2, the maximum-sized vessel that can just squeeze through the Panama Canal.

pilot: imposed, sometimes helpful guide for maneuvering into and leaving a harbor; usually a job sought by retired sea captains. When aboard, a half red, half white flag is flown; when one is requested, a blue and yellow one.

piloting: determining position within sight of land by triangulation from known landmarks or navigational markers.

points of a compass: 32 in circle; or 11.25° (Appendix D).

port: the left side facing forward; once, the dock side of moored ships since right handed sailors kept their steerboards (starboard) outboard when docking. Traditionally, cabin numbers begin at the bow with odd numbers on the starboard side, even numbers to port.

purchase: the free end of a block and tackle, or not so free object from the gift shop.

purser: the man with the purse; business, financial, etc.

rafting: ships tying abreast each other to the same mooring.

RO/RO: as in row, row your boat; a large roll-on, roll-off ship with huge ramps at side or stern for easy transport of wheeled containers and cargo. Not unlike large sea ferries into which they are often converted, and from the ferries in turn, occasionally into cruise ships..

scupper: a sailor's gutter for funneling deck water overboard at the decks edge.

sheer: to a sailor, the rise toward the bow of a ship; a see-through blouse ashore.

ship's period: the characteristic roll period of a ship based on its geometry and metacentric height.

slip: the body of water between two piers; less commonly found today, also a woman's day-wear nightie.

son of a gun: a rascally expression of endearment or awe, but once a pejorative attributing one's origin to the dark area between the guns on the gundecks of warships where, when in port, ladies found room to entertain the sailors who, if allowed ashore, would jump ship.

spring lines: forward or aft diagonally leading mooring lines to keep ship from moving forward or aft.

stabilizer: gyroscopically sensed anti-rolling apparatus which opposes the ship's natural rolling motion.

starboard: from early-on , right handed sailors used "steering boards" or oars mounted on the right side of the ship, facing forward; now starboard instead of "steerboard" side.

stateroom: a pricey cabin.

stem: the prow or forward end of a ship.

stern: the aft end of a ship.

tar: sailor appellation after their custom borrowed from Chinese of tarring their pigtails (and their boats, too).

tender: the not always accessible, not so tender, ship-to-shore boat.

thwart: a seat across the width of a small boat, or narrow door that blocks entry to bath.

topside: out on deck.

tumble home: a ship's sides narrower at Main Deck level than at the waterline; also staggering back from a night ashore.

wharf: where ships tie up parallel to the shore at journey's end.

INDEX

Any comments, corrections, or suggestions will be welcomed by both authors and publisher; please direct correspondence to the attention of the authors at the below address.

Additional copies may be obtained from the distributor, Pacific Pipeline, Inc., from the Disability Bookshop Catalogue of Twin Peaks Press (800) 637-2256 (for orders only), from Bookmasters (800) 247-6553, or alternatively, from the publisher below (Florida residents, please also add 6% sales tax). Please allow 4 weeks for delivery.

Quality Books, Inc. and Unique Books, Inc. will also distribute books to libraries only.

WHEELS AWEIGH PUBLISHING COMPANY
17105 San Carlos Blvd., Suite A-6107
Fort Myers Beach, FL 33931
FAX: (813) 463-5306